YOU NEED TO BE A LITTLE

Crazy

THE TRUTH ABOUT

STARTING AND

GROWING YOUR

BUSINESS

Rich —

BARRY J. MOLTZ

Read this book + get crazy!

Dearborn™
Trade Publishing
A **Kaplan Professional** Company

Vice President and Publisher: Cynthia A. Zigmund
Acquisitions Editor: Jonathan Malysiak
Senior Managing Editor: Jack Kiburz
Interior Design: Lucy Jenkins
Cover Design: Design Solutions
Typesetting: Elizabeth Pitts

Published by Dearborn Trade Publishing
A Kaplan Professional Company

Printed in the United States of America

03 04 05 10 9 8 7 6 5 4 3 2

Library of Congress Cataloging-in-Publication Data

Moltz, Barry J.
    You need to be a little crazy : the truth about starting and growing your business / by Barry J. Moltz.
        p. cm.
"A Kaplan Professional Company."
    ISBN 0-7931-8018-X (6 × 9 paperback)
    1. New business enterprises. 2. Entrepreneurship. 3. Success in business. I. Title.
    HD62.5.M64 2003
    658.1′1–dc21
                                                    2003014116

Dearborn Trade books are available at special quantity discounts to use for sales promotions, employee premiums, or educational purposes. Please call our Special Sales Department to order or for more information at 800-245-2665, e-mail trade@dearborn.com, or write to Dearborn Trade Publishing, 30 South Wacker Drive, Suite 2500, Chicago, IL 60606-7481.

Advance Praise for *You Need to Be a Little Crazy*

"Actually, you'd have to be crazy NOT to start your own business! The truth is that there's nothing more satisfying or productive. Barry's book is a great place to start."
—Seth Godin, Author of *Permission Marketing* and *Purple Cow*

"If you're thinking about starting a business, you'd be crazy not to read this book."
— Daniel H. Pink, Author of *Free Agent Nation*

"Barry Moltz has written an entertaining and important book for anyone who has ever been consumed by the irrepressible creative fever of the high-risk entrepreneur."
—Wendy Goldman Rohm, Author of *The Microsoft File*

"Provides an unvarnished look at the heights and depths surrounding entrepreneurial endeavors as seen from an experienced professional."
—Harold Welsch, Head of DePaul University Entrepreneurship Program

"Entrepreneurship now has its own Bill Cosby. Barry lets us into his private life and private mind to reveal [entrepreneurial] truths in a human way."
—Barry Merkin, Professor of Entrepreneurship, Kellogg School of Business, Northwestern University

"Moltz truly paints a candid portrait of the life of the entrepreneur. If you are an entrepreneur wannabe, this book will test your resolve through its tales of the frustrations, challenges, and sacrifices endured by most entrepreneurs. If you are already an entrepreneur, this book makes you realize you are not alone on your journey and offers advice and support in moving forward."
—Ellen A. Rudnick, Executive Director and Clinical Professor, Michael P. Polsky Center for Entrepreneurship, University of Chicago Graduate School of Business

"Barry Moltz's commonsense approach that includes lessons learned from so many other successful entrepreneurs is a must-read for anyone contemplating starting a business, running or working in a start-up, or reflecting on their own entrepreneurial experiences."
—Linda Salchenberger, Associate Dean, School of Business Administration, and Director, Center for Information Management and Technology, Loyola University Chicago

"This book really delivers what it promises: the absolute truth, straight from the horse's mouth, about getting your own business off the ground. It's not for the faint of heart, but if you are truly driven by a passion to start your own business, *You Need to Be a Little Crazy* is a must-read!"
—Roger Luman, Managing Director, Turner Center for Entrepreneurship

"Entrepreneurship is much more than a set of tools and techniques for starting and growing a business. Barry's book discusses all facets of entrepreneurship that capture the never-ending roller-coaster ride of launching and building businesses. This is a must-read that goes beyond the inside operations of new venture creation and gives us a rich account of the passion, values, and struggles of today's entrepreneur."
> —Jill Kickul, Elizabeth J. McCandless Professor of Entrepreneurship, Simmons School of Management

"Barry Moltz was in Nike mode when he wrote *You Need to Be a Little Crazy*, repeatedly telling his audience of would-be entrepreneurs, 'Just do it!' Don't worry about what others think, whether the stars are properly aligned, whether there might be a better time, or whether you'll get rich. Just do it. Because, as Moltz underlines repeatedly, until you take the leap and launch your own business, there is no way to know. This book is well worth your time."
> —George Lipper, National Association of Seed and Venture Funds

"Barry Moltz pulls no punches as he describes the tremendous highs and lows of starting a business. By relating his own experiences as an entrepreneur, as well as the experiences of scores of others, Barry has distilled universal truths that every start-up entrepreneur can learn—and benefit—from. Lively, sobering, realistic, informative, and at times inspiring, *You Need to Be a Little Crazy* is a book you definitely need to read before taking the life-changing step of becoming an entrepreneur."
> —Brian Hill, Coauthor of *Attracting Capital from Angels* and the Corporate Thriller *Overtime*

"Moltz is right on the money in his new book, *You Need to Be a Little Crazy*. His perspective as both a businessperson and an investor gives budding entrepreneurs a clear picture of the challenges that lay ahead when starting a business. The personal insight Moltz provides is enlightening—and invaluable."
> —Dee Power, Author of *Inside Secrets to Venture Capital*

"To the fledgling or would-be entrepreneur, *You Need to Be a Little Crazy* is a huge dose of reality. Read it quickly. Underline all the signposts of the rocky road ahead, then forge ahead with a newly informed passion. To those of us who have already launched and sustained new businesses, Barry's book helps explain all our wild, tumultuous feelings. Most importantly, by reading this book, we can join the community of friends who persist in trudging along this strange path and lose our terminal sense of uniqueness."
> —Clay Garner, President, Growth Resources Inc., Chairman–Chicago, TEC International

"Barry Moltz has created a groundbreaking book that inspires people into powerful action to grow a successful business. Funny, provocative, and always engaging, he is a master storyteller."
> —Melissa Giovagnoli, President, Networlding, and Coauthor of *Networlding* and *The Power of Two: How Companies of All Sizes Can Build Alliance Networks That Generate Business Opportunities*

For my wife, Sara, who has stood by me through this journey, sometimes against her better judgment.

For my sons who showed me light even on the darkest days.

And for the entrepreneurs who courageously rise every morning to run their businesses.

"The kind of adventure I am talking about, once you've launched, never really ends. To succeed requires perseverance as well as nerve, savvy as well as innocence, plus the ability to focus single-mindedly, plus a kind of damn-I'm-going-to-do-this-no-matter-what-it-takes confidence. In sum, you have to be a little crazy."

Bold Women, Big Ideas
Kay Koplovitz
with Peter Israel

"It's the romance, not the finance that makes business worth pursuing."

The Monk and the Riddle
Randy Komisar
with Kent Lineback

I want to first thank Sally Duros. Without her, this book would not have been possible. When I met Sally in 2002, my thoughts of writing a book were a mess of ideas. Through her guidance and taped interviews, we were able to organize my ramblings and make this book a reality. Her constant probing of the material brought out the best in my writing and philosophy. Everyone who was interviewed and profiled by Sally for this book was impressed with her professionalism and passion for this project.

I want to thank my best friend, Zane Smith, who is also a personal injury attorney in Chicago. He was there in the mid-1990s during very difficult times providing support when I needed it most. He also gave the working title for the book, when he told me during a tough business period, "Barry, the worst they can do is eat you, and that's illegal."

Thank you to Dave Lundy at Aileron Communications and a columnist for the *Chicago Sun-Times*. He was the first one to write about my passion for entrepreneurship and made me realize I had a story to tell.

Thank you to my acquisitions editor, Jon Malysiak, at Dearborn Trade Publishing, who had the faith and confidence to publish a first-time author like me.

Thanks to those who gave me the time and space to write this on most Fridays over the past year. My family let me hide in my office in the basement for endless hours. Thanks to Kat French at Spa Space in Chicago for healing my cramped body after hours of writing at the computer. Thanks to Jessica for introducing me to Ali Farka Toure, who became the only musician I could listen to when I wrote this book.

Thanks to my parents, Alan and Carole, who instilled in me the confidence to try to succeed in everything I did. Thanks to my Seido Karate teachers at Thousand Waves, Kyoshi Nancy Lanoue and Sensei

Sarah Ludden, who have taught me the meaning of *osu*–to continue to strive with patience.

Finally, thanks to Mike Cooper, may he rest in peace, who was that person who really taught me how much fun business can be.

Having been an entrepreneur for more than 30 years, I believe that you never stop learning about the challenges of starting new businesses and that you can learn something from almost anyone. The trick is to learn important and valuable things from the right people. People who've done it before, and, more important, people who've had and who've taken the time to think about the process—its highs, its lows, and all its warts. Barry Moltz is one of those people. Engaged on a daily basis in every aspect of building and managing new businesses, and a successful entrepreneur and venture investor in his own right, he works with owners and managers directly on the front lines.

In today's marketplace of ideas and brain-based businesses, information is abundant, but wisdom and relevant experience are increasingly harder to come by. It's difficult these days to separate what's true from what's simply popular. Too many onetime wonders are now business experts writing cookbooks that litter the bookshelves but add very little to the ongoing serious discussions. We're all pretty weary of war stories—especially from second- and third-rate warriors. I figure if you're going to invest your money and your even scarcer time in reading a book, you should make sure it matters.

When I first met Barry Moltz, I was struck by his unique perspective on the trials and tribulations of entrepreneurship. He took as a given all the typical questions and concerns (about deal making, valuation issues, control concerns, etc.) and turned instead to the much more interesting and harder personal issues. Identity. Family. Failure. These aren't soft subjects and it's not easy talking about what no one wants to hear. But that doesn't make them any less important.

Identity is important because entrepreneurs constantly confuse what they do with who they are. We're all certainly responsible for what we do but failing doesn't make us bad people and succeeding doesn't make us omniscient.

Family is important because it's a much more important extension of ourselves than any work we'll ever do. There's always more work but you've only got one family.

And failure's important because the first time you win (or lose), it could be luck, it could be timing, or it could be talent. It's only after you fail once or twice and learn to rely equally on thought, analysis, and anticipation—in addition to speed, talent, and execution—that you can really call yourself an entrepreneur. This is why there are so few successful second acts from entrepreneurs. In the long run, it's mind over muscle, strategy over strength, and a healthy perspective—not just a lot of perspiration—that make someone a real success in his or her business and in the equally important rest of his or her life.

The advice in this book may not always be the "flavor of the month," but it's realistic and true. It may not be all starry-eyed and inspirational, but then neither is life. And it may not even be what you want to hear—whether you're starting out on your first business venture or wrapping up your 15th—but it's important to know nonetheless.

So, as Yogi Berra used to say, "When you come to a fork in the road, take it." And as you start off on your new business journey, take this book along with you. You couldn't have a better guide.

Howard Tullman
Serial Entrepreneur and President of Kendall College
Evanston, Illinois
May 2003

I am by most of our society's defini-
tions an entrepreneur although I have never been comfortable with that
word. It sounds far too romantic for what the owner of a small business
does. Sure, some people begin by dreaming of an idea and planning it
carefully. But mostly we fall into our businesses by circumstance. We
then scrape, claw, and beg for money from our families and friends to
get our businesses going. Once we get started, we work day and night to
build a product and sell it to customers. If we are lucky, someone buys
what we are selling at a profit, and we can make a living. If we are very
lucky, maybe, just maybe, someone buys our business someday and we
have an additional payday. But most of the time, we go through every
day working hard to keep our customers happy, to make our businesses
profitable, and to support our families.

If I wanted to hold a regular job I would. But after enjoying an initial successful career with IBM, I haven't had a job working for someone
else since 1991. Something that drives me inside wants to see my ideas
succeed or fail. I have never been much of a follower although I like to
learn. I don't take well to authority but I do like rules.

The reader should make no mistake; it is easier and in the long run
more profitable to get a job than to start your own business. If you want
to have your own business for the money, then forget it: go get a job.
That motivation will never sustain you through the ups and downs of
starting and building your business. Entrepreneurs start businesses because, like an actor's dreams of stardom, they have no choice. Passion
and energy drive them on the good days and sustain them on the bad
ones.

I started my career as a political science graduate from Brandeis
University in 1981. Three days before I graduated from college, IBM offered me a job in Chicago that was 1,000 miles from home. It paid
$18,900. A recession was going on. I had nothing to do on the Monday

after graduation. I cut my hair, shaved my beard, got a blue suit and white shirt, and took the job. Two weeks later, I moved to Chicago and started my career at Big Blue. I loved it. I had a new group of friends, a studio apartment on the lake, two suits, and money in my pocket. IBM taught me about computers, how to sell, and how to be a good corporate citizen. For the next nine years, I succeeded at most of the things IBM asked me to do, and was promoted almost every year. I met my future wife in 1988 and told her I would be president of IBM someday. How did she feel about living in Armonk, New York, where the company head-quarters was located? I was climbing the corporate ladder of success just like I thought I would.

What this experience did not prepare me for was my step out of the corporate world and into the new world of small business. One of my IBM customers at the time was a small, growing consulting firm, Whitt-man-Hart. One of its founders, Bob Bernard, would later go on in the 1990s (without me) to build a billion-dollar public firm called March-First. Bob introduced me to the fast-paced exciting world of small busi-ness. After nine years at IBM, I was looking for more responsibility and less structure.

At about the same time, I had read Paul Hawken's book, *Growing a Business,* and it captivated my attention. I had previously started a small business selling advertising for a directory we called *Yes, We Deliver.* In these pre-Internet days of 1988, there was no good way to find all the places that delivered. I created one with my friends and girlfriend. I worked hard on this part-time while at IBM, but after a year, we closed it. Still, I had been bitten by the entrepreneur's bug.

So I left IBM in 1990 to become Director of Sales for Whittman-Hart. I traded in my blue suits for top designer Hugo Boss clothes and collected my six-figure paycheck. My new office had a high-back green leather chair, teak furniture, and a laser jet printer, and I had my own private assistant, Denise.

I dove into the shallow end of small business and belly flopped. After having spent nine years at IBM, I lasted only a year at Whittman-Hart before I was fired in 1991. I was ill-prepared for the fast-paced, cutthroat environment of a much smaller organization. The company, inside and outside, seemed to have no rules. It certainly had no 75-year-old guidelines to follow.

The company was run firmly by Bob Bernard, who was now its sole remaining founder as well as president and CEO. This was really the first time I saw how the owner's decisions and style influenced everything about life on a daily basis inside and outside the company. Bob had a great sense of fashion. I heard at the time he owned 40 or more suits. It was a fashion show at the office every day, with men dressing better than the women. We all wanted to show off our new Hugo Boss ties and Giorgio Armani suits. I was thankful to Bob for my new wardrobe. Even today I think of him when I can still dress up in style.

So during the recession of 1991, I was booted out the door to begin my entrepreneurial adventures. Over the next ten years, I experienced most of what can happen by having your own company. In my second business, I was kicked out by my two partners. In my third business (luckily for my marriage's sake), I sold during the Internet bubble of 1999. I escaped my last business with my family life and financial well-being mostly intact. What I lost and gained along the way is the tale I am telling.

1

YOU

It's All in Your Mind

STRENGTH AND COURAGE

I remember in the mid-1990s, a friend had given me a carved medallion on a rope with strange symbols and markings on the front. When I turned it over, a scrawled inscription simply read "To Give Strength and Courage." In a weird way, the word *Strength* was hyphenated between two lines, defying all rules of grammar. At the time, I thought it a nice gift, but not much more. Months later when things were going particularly bad for me in business, I remember stumbling across it in a drawer, pulling it out, and putting it around my neck. I thought this might help me get through a day when I was at "the bottom of the roller coaster." I was desperate, and I would try anything.

While starting and running businesses over the past 15 years, some days I never wanted to end. The orders would roll in and growth seemed endless. New customers would call up and beg for business. Other days were nightmares. No one wanted to buy what we were selling at any price. We were begging for customers. On top of this, my best employee would leave, the phone system would go down, and we could not ship any orders because the computer system had crashed. I couldn't wait for that day to end. How do I answer my wife when I get home, and she asks, "How was your day, honey?"

After this kind of day, I would rise the next day and go into the office fearful of what might come next. In some strange way the medallion helped me. I would pull it out, run my fingers across the inscription and think to myself, *strength and courage.* I would focus on surviving just for that one day. For today, I reasoned, this one small goal would be good enough.

S o m e t i m e s   t o   **S** u r v i v e   **I** s   **E** n o u g h

COURAGE IS THE ENTREPRENEURIAL LAW

Many people would call the entrepreneur brave for starting his or her own business. It does take courage but this is too simplistic. Purple hearts are not given out for starting a business or struggling to make a business work. Yet starting a business does require a lot of forethought.

Actually, it is a lot less glamorous than that. Writer Samuel Johnson said: "Courage is the greatest of all virtues, because if you haven't courage, you may not have an opportunity to use any of the others." Although courage may be the starting point, it takes more than courage to be an entrepreneur. Why would anyone in his or her right mind leave a job that gives you a paycheck every week to start a business that statistically is doomed to fail? The Office of Advocacy at the Small Business Administration (SBA) says that 33 percent of all businesses fail in their first two years and more than 50 percent close in the first four years. The SBA states that 584,500 businesses closed in 2002 alone.

Given these statistics, even with established businesses being not as stable as they were 20 years ago, why would people leave health insurance, paid vacation, and a good retirement plan for a long shot like that?

Most small businesses fail during the first five years. The simple reason is the business runs out of cash. The business closes because there is no longer money to operate it. The owner has more unpaid bills than money coming in from his customers. More generally, over time, the entrepreneur either failed to identify a problem that customers would pay him to solve or competitors found this to be a lucrative niche and entered the market with their products. At this point, the entrepreneur might not have had an advantage to beat this new competition. As a result, the business landscape changed. Alternatively, the business owner may have been good at starting the business but did not have the skills to grow it. There is really no way to ever find out why your business failed, so don't get caught up analyzing it. This is a futile effort. No matter what you do, you can't prevent the failure or ensure the success of your business, so stop trying.

It's Only a Starting Point

SO WHY DO WE DO IT?

Because so many start-up businesses fail, why do so many of us act irrationally as lunatics and start businesses? Why are more than half a million businesses started every year?

We are constantly bombarded by media messages about the "good life" of being rich and famous. We want a "better life" for our families and ourselves. Best-sellers and magazines tell us that we should chase our dream. These images constantly glitter and attract us. In our society, this is in stark contrast to the day-to-day reality of commuting to a job and a company environment that rarely seems to change. Sure, with a job we get a reliable weekly paycheck, the promise of a funded retirement, and the "coveted" gold watch, but for many of us, the boredom sets in as we become good at our jobs. While we are driving or taking the train to work, we have an opportunity to think about whether there is more to life and a professional career than this. Around us we hear the rags-to-riches stories. Financial business successes are glorified in our culture, and we think we can be "one of them." Financially successful businesspeople like Bill Gates, Michael Dell, and Donald Trump have become our modern-day heroes.

We think that the "grass is always greener on the other side." We may even begin to dislike our bosses, our customers, or our coworkers to justify our feelings. We want to pursue a hobby or dream professionally. We tell ourselves that we want to "work for ourselves." We have "always" wanted to do this or be that, so why not now?

This happened a lot in the late 1990s during the Internet bubble when seemingly "everybody was making money" and we did not want to get left behind. We act irrationally out of a desperate fear that a better, more financially fulfilling life is passing us by.

We then either quit our jobs or find ourselves laid off without a job. An adventure that we are surely not prepared for begins. We are armed only with our dream, passion, or desire. As with most things, this dream never quite matches up with reality. The fantasy is always a heck of a lot more fun than the grind of daily life. But inside these visions and dreams is exactly where the joy starts and the passion for launching the business begins to resonate.

W e A re M oved by O ur D esires

"The simple truth is that once I get a big, potent idea, it moves me to distraction. I feel compelled to move others with me. . . . Perhaps there's something seductive for me in traveling into the unknown. The journey itself thrills me, and I don't think I'd ever feel altogether happy if I didn't know there was risk involved."

Kay Koplovitz

YOU MUST BE CRAZY

It does take courage, but it actually takes being a lunatic to start a company against such great odds. Simply stated, you must be crazy.

A lunatic is defined in the dictionary as someone who is insane or eccentric. Additionally, a lunatic is often described as wildly and giddily foolish.

That's right. To start a business you must be nuts.

Admit this and you have made a good start. But you need to be a certain kind of lunatic. You need to be a lunatic who has a steadfast long-term belief in her vision—a lunatic who will try anything, ask anyone for everything, and see everyone as a source of help. You also need to be comfortable being alone in your beliefs because the only thing others will agree with you on is that you are indeed crazy.

Only someone who is crazy can survive the ups and downs that a business brings. Pick yourself up, brush yourself off, and move on. It's a start.

And a **S**urvivor

"It's in your blood. That is just who you are. When you are an entrepreneur you are the puzzle. It is hard to just use a portion of what you have."

Suzi Bonk

DON'T WASTE YOUR COURAGE

During the 1990s Internet bubble, things were more premeditated. Many of us pursued business ideas with the sole goal of getting rich. It didn't matter that we knew nothing about the particular field of business or whether someone would actually pay us to solve this specific problem. What mattered was whether outside angel investors or venture capitalists (collectively called Other People's Money, or OPM for short) would give us money so we could pay ourselves to pursue this opportunity. Our expectations were to get a few million dollars, lease some great office space, hire some cool people with great titles, and buy some fancy office furniture with a foosball table. Nothing else mattered, because the market told us we would be rich in 18 months after our company went public, and we sold an initial public offering of stock. It seemed that you almost could write a business plan one weekend, start the company on Monday, and go public on Friday. Then you had all weekend to party with your newfound wealth! These ideas are well outlined by Silicon Valley sage and entrepreneur Randy Komisar in his 2001 book, *The Monk and the Riddle,* in which he helps a fictional Lenny who wants to find venture capital funding for his online casket-selling business. Lenny has no previous experience in this market but reasons that it must be a good business for people are dying all the time.

During the bubble, companies with only an idea and a business plan were obtaining billions of dollars in funding. These companies were spending millions of dollars on things like Super Bowl ads with sock puppets. These upstarts had few sales, but still they were able to IPO and raise millions of dollars. Their market capitalization was worth more than many brick-and-mortar companies trading on the stock market. In many cases, established companies such as Barnes & Noble had dot-com spin-offs like Barnesandnoble.com that were valued at almost as much as the founding company.

This frenzy led Andrew Flipowski, CEO of Divine Interventures (now Divine, Inc.), in February 2000 to predict that Sears and General Electric would be out of business in a year. With firms like CMGI capitalized at $50 billion, Flipowski predicted that his company as well as other Internet incubators would top the Fortune 500. In 2003, Divine, Inc. filed for bankruptcy, and assets of the company are being sold off. CMGI trades for about a dollar a share, and its market capitalization is worth millions of dollars instead of billions of dollars. General Electric retains a market capitalization of more than $275 billion.

This was the time of selling pet food online where shipping orders cost more than the products themselves. American business did not care about profit. Speed, size, and glitz were the major drivers. I drank the Kool-Aid like everyone else, and I enjoyed it.

Sadly, many people left well-paying jobs and good careers to catch a brass ring that never materialized after the bubble burst in 2000. In fact, a shirt that I bought at this time simply stated, "I worked at a start-up and all I got was this T-shirt!"

The 1990s was that part of the American dream that wanted to get rich quick. This part of the dream is where we look for every shortcut there is to avoid putting in the required time or effort to get there. As much as an ethic of hard work and building something slowly over time is part of the dream, another part of the dream is to leverage Lady Luck and strike it rich by taking shortcuts. This not only leads to many people committing crimes (and in turn doing time), but to a lot of unrealistic expectations about how to get there.

The Get-Rich-Quick Schemes Are Over

"I have calculated that we financially would have been better off if we'd stayed where we were, as of right now. There's truth to it; you've got to be crazy."

"People start a business because they're mad: they want to quit their jobs. But what they really want is—they don't want to have a boss. That's very different from saying, 'I'm going to go build a business.'"

"Truthfully, most people can make a lot more money just being a successful freelancer or a successful sole proprietorship than working for somebody else. But to build a business means you have to sacrifice a great deal of that for a long period of time, because what you're trying to do is build a business that is not dependent on you. You are developing equity value in it."

Mike Duda

IF YOU WANT MONEY, FIND A JOB

So forget about starting or running a business now in the 2000s as a get-rich-quick scheme. If you want to financially keep up with your friends, make lots of money, or accumulate wealth, get a job. Starting a business is not for those who only want to make money. You have more of a chance during the first five years of business to make a great living by working for someone else than by working for yourself. With a job, you will still be living the American dream: a predictable paycheck, a house in the suburbs for your family, and two cars in your garage. There is nothing wrong with this. In fact, on many days, I wished I preferred this and could go do it. To me, in some ways this really does sound like a dream come true.

Sean Lundgren who runs a Web-based DVD and video business struggles to financially make ends meet. He barely has enough to support his family. Bill collectors call him all the time so he needs to screen every call. They even found his wife's number at her place of employment. It is difficult for him to watch his friends with good-paying jobs buy new cars and nice clothes and go on family vacations. He questions his decision to stay on the path of running his own business as he falls farther and farther behind in "keeping up with the Joneses."

Your Start-Up Can Still Be Your Dream

"I was naïve to think it would be easy to succeed. Sometimes, things are so scary and overwhelming. Here I am competing with world-class conglomerates. So far, I am not in the loony bin. I rather refer to it as climbing a mountain."

Vicki Esralew

YOU MIGHT JUST WIND UP THERE

If you had to think about it, you probably would not undertake such an adventure as starting a business. Use common sense and some thoughtful analysis, but let the passion and the market drive your business launch. Some of the most successful business people start a new company because they "find themselves there." They are kicked out of their last job, and someone has asked them to do something for them for which they can get paid. Jack Miller, former President of Quill Corporation, talks about why he started his office supply business. "I had to make a living," he says. He started his office supply business in his dad's chicken store in 1956. In 1998, 42 years later, he and his brothers, Harvey and Arnold, sold the company to Staples for $690 million.

You should not start a business just because you are unhappy in your job. Maybe you should look for another job, get a new boss, or take a different position. Pursue these things first before adventuring out. Luckily, starting your own business these days is not the thing to do. In the 1990s during the Internet gold rush, many people left their jobs to start a company. Most of these "tourists" have gone back to work, some even returning to the same company.

A good example of this is Jim Lichtenstein who was a managing editor at CBS Channel 2 in Chicago. He left his position in October 2000 to launch AssignmentEditor.com full-time. Two years and more than $1 million of investors' money later, he sold the company at a loss. Once an entrepreneur, he is now looking to return to the newsroom.

Entrepreneurship Is Not a Tourist Industry

"It is hard, and at some point . . . well, I'll go back and work for somebody again. [Starting the business] was getting it out of [my] system, too. Years ago, I wanted to be a movie producer, and OK, I went and did that. Then I wanted to work in entertainment television, and I did that. Then I thought it would be cool to start a business, and so I did that. Now, well, is there anything else I really want to do, or do I just want to go someplace and have good health insurance and a stock plan and all that stuff? It's OK, that doesn't look so bad anymore."

Jim Lichtenstein

IF YOU CHOOSE WHAT YOU LOVE

The title of a book in the 1980s stated *Do What You Love, the Money Will Follow.* I never read the book and I am sure that the title doesn't tell the whole story. But I always thought this phrase was kind of silly and arrogant. I can think of plenty of things that I love to do, and the money surely would not follow. Who would pay me to sing for them when the only two places that I have ever sung are the shower and the car? I know I could sing for whomever I wanted and just as surely the money would never follow. It may make sense to pursue being a singer as a hobby, but not as a business.

I would prefer to think that if you have the financial luxury, you should "Do what you love even if the money does not follow." We all face economic realities. We have to support ourselves and perhaps our families. Many people work in a job or earn a living from something they do not love. This may be an economic fact of your life. You should still follow your business passion, however, even if you can only moonlight at it.

Also, be careful about starting a business to pursue a hobby you love. Very few people can make a living from their hobby or a favorite interest. I cringe sometimes when I ask people why they started a particular business and they say, "Well, I love to eat out, and I always wanted to own a restaurant." I tell them that they can have a lot of fun keeping their day job and eating at restaurants instead of starting one! This is one reason why two-thirds of all retail stores close within a year of opening. Liking an area of business and knowing how to run a business in that area are two different things. This is why franchises are not a bad alternative for some people for they give you a road map and other tools to run the business. Even in a franchise, for example, Kinko's, the reality of using the services of one and running one are very different.

Money **I**s **N**ot **R**equired *to* **F**ollow

START-UPS ARE MY DRUG OF CHOICE

Besides the fact that we're crazy, why in the world do so many of us start businesses if the odds are already stacked against us? I think you may already know why if you have listened to the tales of your friends and listened to that voice inside yourself. I remember in 1993 when I started my last business, my father begged me not to do it and to instead get a "real job."

As he saw it, after having left a very successful and rewarding career at IBM in the 1980s, I had run into one disaster after another. I was fired from my job at Whittman-Hart a year after taking it. My first entrepreneurial venture went out of business a year after we started. Customers liked our idea, but we could not get enough of them to support ourselves. In my second business, I was kicked out by the two original partners one year after we started. My father couldn't understand why I would want to do it again. He said to me one evening, "Think, Barry, Sara is pregnant. You have a child on the way. It is time to get serious again about supporting them. It's time to go back and get a job. Things went so well for you at IBM. Maybe they will take you back."

At the time, I didn't have a good answer for him. To be honest, his arguments made sense. The only thing I could do was shut down the reasoning part of my brain. I started my third business a few weeks after my first son was born. Years later, I realize that I can't help myself. Like an actor on the stage or a minor league baseball player on the field, I have no choice but to pursue my passion. In my case, the passion is business ideas and trying to make them work.

Many times, I think that I am incapable of working for someone else. My last manager at IBM ruined that for me, just as Bob Bernard at Whittman-Hart ignited the entrepreneurial flame inside of me. For better or for worse, I have no choice but to live in the entrepreneurial world.

I should admit all this and confess: I am an entrepreneurholic. I am powerless to control myself. This is how I get my kicks. This is what drives me. Maybe it's because I gave up drinking and smoking, and this is all I have left to add excitement to my life. Luckily, somehow, so far, over the long term, I always make more money than I lose so I can support my family and continue this crazy cycle. I also have a very understanding wife who has enough faith and confidence in me after 15 years of this type of trip to indulge and support me in these efforts. I know they don't give out medals for starting and running a business, but they should. If I were given one, I would pin it on my wife (and be careful not to stick her again!).

Entrepreneurship Is a Disease

"I felt that it is my blessing, privilege, and responsibility as a parent [to create these products]. There are so many wonderful companies that have unbelievable resources. I had zero. Personal belief and passion propelled me."

Vicki Esralew

PASSION IS THE DNA

I think your optimism drives you, but it is your passion that keeps you going. You will have only this passion to hold on to and sustain you during the really bad times. The good times will strengthen this passion so you can again survive other downturns that will surely come your way. Forget using money and the brass ring to ground you when starting or running a business. That motivation will not survive the first downturn. The financial goal will seem too distant, and you will go crawling back to your last employer wondering why you ever left.

During my difficult business times, I always knew that my passion was to see my ideas succeed or fail.

When things go well, your passion propels you almost blindly forward, sometimes with an overwhelming fervor. You may feel out of control as this boundless enthusiasm blinds you. Your passion also may take the form of an anger to accomplish something despite the odds. Passion will give you energy and power. It recharges you on those tough days. But it can also cause you to doubt your motivation during difficult times. You may view passion as your enemy within. You may wonder whether your ideas are "too crazy." You may wonder whether your ideas are "ahead of your time."

We forget the statistics. We forget all the advice. We think this business idea is a sure thing, and we want to go for it. Entrepreneurs are not risk takers. They are dreamers. They can't always appreciate or measure the risk that they are about to take. I certainly had no idea when I started my businesses, what the level of risk was for myself, my health, my family, and my family's financial assets. I wasn't taking a calculated risk, I was dreaming of what I could build.

You need to dream. Those of us who do not dream get nightmares. You will experience enough of those during the day running your own business.

P assion C an A lso F eel L ike the E nemy W ithin

HOW DO YOU CATCH THE PASSION?

How do entrepreneurs get this passion? Are you born with it? One day, you find yourself there. After graduating from college in 1981 and being recruited by IBM, I thought I would be with this company forever. The blue suits, white shirts, and red ties were for me. I wanted to work my way up and become president of IBM! So how did this change? I had been promoted almost every year at IBM and had won many awards. IBM taught me about computers and how to sell. I liked the people I worked with and the ethical culture the company promoted.

The life-changing experience for me was meeting two people in the late 1980s. The first person was an IBM branch manager. I had little respect for him. He had risen quickly up the promotion ladder, and he looked the part, but I did not think he was effective. He played the political games well, but he did not care about the customer or his team. I felt that he promoted friendship over business merit, and I wanted no part of this. He often held sales contests, and the first prize was lunch with him. I always wondered whether second prize would be two lunches with him?

The second person was Bob Bernard, a soon-to-be-famous entrepreneur who had started a small consulting company a few years earlier. I was impressed by what he had achieved and where he was going. Years later he offered me a job as head of his national sales force. Feeling that I had hit the wall at IBM, I jumped at Bob's offer. Ironically, I learned that the manager I had disliked at IBM, in a twist of fate, had also gone to work for Bob Bernard in the late 1990s. This was long after I had left.

Like many people, I started my businesses mostly because I had no choice. After leaving IBM, and being fired from my first job after that, I could not go back to the corporate world. Every job interview I had at the time confirmed this feeling inside of me. I had tasted small business through my time at Whittman-Hart and wanted to start my own thing.

You Need to Do Your Own Thing

"If you knew everything you would be encountering on your path to building your business, there is no way you would ever start."

"Passion is not something you experience. It is in you. It makes you get up in the morning and shout 'Whoo! Hoo!' because you really want to tackle that day ahead of you. It is that high when you look around a room of people and you think these people are here because they really believe in what you have built."

"Passion is when you are losing your biggest client and you are looking at your cash flow. You are thinking, Oh my, how will I meet payroll next month, but then you go out, and you find another client, and another client."

"Passion keeps you calling. Passion keeps you moving. It keeps you smiling and keeps you energized because you love [doing what you are doing] so much. It is never about the money. Passion pulls you through."

Marsha McVicker

ENTREPRENEURS ARE GENETICALLY OPTIMISTIC

In 2002, I heard Bill Reichert, Managing Director of Garage Technology Ventures, tell his audience that entrepreneurs are "genetically optimistic." He felt this was the only possible reason someone would start and run a business. In many respects, I agree with Bill. If you were not somewhat delusional, you would probably realize that your statistical chances of succeeding are small and you should remain with your job.

But even with the proper genetic makeup, you won't be an entrepreneur unless you take the leap and seek your edge. Some people have wanted to be entrepreneurs their whole lives. Not me. I had wanted to be a rabbi, a lawyer, or president of IBM. Like many other kids, I had my own paper route (which my father ran with me most of the time). I sold stuff for school and the Boy Scouts. But coming out of college, I always wanted to work for a large company. I liked the structure, and nine years at IBM were the result. But during this time, I gained confidence in my ability and lost faith in my managers. The entrepreneurial drive to do it myself bubbled up in me. Working for Bob Bernard at Whittman-Hart sealed it. Now when I see my young son set up a store in front of our house so he can sell stuff from his room I wonder whether he will be driven to a similar entrepreneurial fate.

Y*ou* C*an't* H*elp* Y*ourself*

PASSION IS A LEAP

There is no perfect time to "become an entrepreneur" or to start a business. You don't get to choose. I started my third business weeks after my first son was born. By any standard, this was not good timing. Somewhere along the line, you simply close your eyes and leap. You consciously propel yourself forward toward that unknown while realizing that you might fall.

Does desire pull you or fear push you to leap? For me, it was a combination of both. I was attracted by what could be in the future and repulsed by what had happened in the past. These things together propelled me forward or at least into a different direction than I had come from. The desire to dream something better combined with the fear of not wanting to look back is potent.

During your leap, you keep your eyes wide open out of sheer excitement and wonder about what may come next. Alternately, you keep your eyes tightly closed to shut out the fear about what might happen.

The desire to see my ideas succeed or fail was very powerful. I had the desire to create something from nothing and make a contribution to life through the business world.

Simultaneously, the fear was having to work for another boss I did not like or having to follow someone else's rules I did not believe in. I was also driven by the fear of not having enough money, and by realizing that I had to make a living to support my family. Another fear was that someday I would receive my gold watch for 25 years of service and look back to see that I had not done what I really wanted to do with my life.

Fear and desire combined make a powerful passion cocktail that can fuel the entrepreneur. That passion can be so attractive that it pushes you forward no matter what your own common sense or your friends might be telling you.

Many of us are forced to leap. For me, the force was not wanting to work for another large corporation or not wanting to work for someone I saw as being an incompetent manager. It was being unemployed and not being able to find a job. It was having just enough money saved to be able to survive on my own for a while without having to get paid.

For me, it was feeling just brave, or, viewed another way, being stupid enough to think that I could succeed at the "starting my own business game." The books I had read on the subject gave me confidence. This turned out to be false bravado for they did not prepare me for anything that was to come. But they did give me the courage to leap. My success at IBM gave me the confidence that I could strike out on my own though nothing I did there prepared me for having my own business. The transition was difficult and the skills were not transferable. But I was just foolish enough to try, and beginning is always the most difficult part.

Once I started, there was no looking or going back. I was committed. But going in, I did believe that I had a safety net, and that no matter what happened I would be OK. I knew that the friends and family who were around me would still love and support me. No matter what happened, I would be able to find a job or earn a living if I had to. My family would not go hungry. This was a powerful realization for me: that I would be OK no matter what. Later while running my own businesses, I became less sure of this.

G*et* R*eady to* J*ump*

YOUR BUSINESS IS YOU SEEKING YOUR EDGE

Standing at the edge is about responsibility and challenge for the entrepreneur. It's about standing there completely naked and exposed to the business elements. It's about being completely vulnerable, and it's about feeling uncomfortable. This is what stirs the deep anxiety in many of us, but it is also what pulls us in the first place.

The challenge of facing unknown elements can be a powerful and exciting motivator. One of my favorite explorers is Ernest Shackleton, who took his men and his ship, *The Endurance,* across Antarctica in 1914. His advertisement in the newspaper seeking men for the voyage, read:

> Men wanted for Hazardous Journey, Small Wages, Bitter Cold, Long Months of Complete Darkness, Constant Danger, Safe Return Doubtful, Honor and Recognition in Case of Success.

This sounds a lot like the journey of starting and running a business. His ship's name was appropriate since he had to endure 286 days frozen in Arctic ice before his men could begin a journey that eventually led them to safety. For Shackleton and his men, simply surviving became the daily goal. It's amazing to note that during this long adventure, he did not lose a single man. Shackleton was not only responsible for getting his men stuck in the ice, but he also nearly single-handedly rescued them.

Finding your edge is about taking personal responsibility. The buck stops with you, and that's OK. This is what you wanted. It is important to remember and retain this once you get other people working for you. Don't shift blame. Ultimately, it's about you, so accept it.

Running a business is not reckless risk taking. It's about finding your inner strength against the business elements. It's about finding exactly where the edge of your identity is. What are you made of exactly? Do you have what it takes to face the unknown and accept new challenges that arise from nowhere? It's about testing yourself and finding out who you really are. It's about realizing what drives you. It's about using that inner strength to bounce back from a setback.

One of my favorite Zen Buddhist expressions is "Fall down seven times, stand up eight times." The hardest part of any journey is getting knocked down the first time. Once you get up, it's a lot easier to get knocked down again, because you know you can take a hit and go on. This is why sparring in my Seido karate training has become so valuable to me. In practice, I know what it feels like to take a hit from another person. So if the situation arises where I need to defend myself, I will know what it feels like when someone strikes me. I can get up, escape, or strike back.

Standing alone against the business elements is not romantic or soul soothing, but it can be rewarding. The natural business world is indifferent. It does not owe you success no matter how hard you work or how much money you have invested. The free market economy simply does not care about your business or anyone else's.

This realization of indifference first chilled me to the bone. I was alone, and the world did not care. All pretense of promising bright futures and glorified past successes are stripped away. The entrepreneur is like Tom Hanks in the movie *Castaway,* who withstands a lot of physical pain as he stands alone against the elements. It is similar to losing someone you love, where a warming color somehow has left the world.

But as an entrepreneur, you are not shipwrecked alone on a deserted island. The free market economy may not care about you, but the team members you work with do. Your family, friends, and mentors will support you on your journey. You may feel like you are on a desert island when you start your business, but you have a high-speed Internet line and a cell phone that you can use to get help. These are the only comforts you really need.

Find Comforts at Your Edge

"Entrepreneurs have a certain mind-set. When you have that mind-set, you can't stand the thought of being back in a corporate setting."

"Entrepreneurship is the story of high-beta life. Very high highs and very low lows. If your personality is well matched with that, well then you can't get enough of it. And if not, well then you don't, and then you're not. And you do not belong there."

"A lot of people crossed over to entrepreneurship and found out that their personalities were not well matched. Now they are b-to-b, back to banking, or b-to-c, back to consulting. Because they are not well suited to be entrepreneurs."

"A lot of us grew up with Depression mommies and daddies, when managing risk meant going to work for a large company and staying there all their lives. That is actually a terrible way to manage risk. When I dove off and swam over to the dark side, it did not exactly pass the mother-in-law test."

"It turned out to be a fabulous experience."

John Banta

SAVE A PERSON, SAVE THE WORLD

That's my passion. This is the essence of why I start and run businesses. It is the way that I can make a difference in other people's lives. Judaism says, "He who saves a single person, saves the entire world." Environmentalists say, "Think globally, act locally." This is not very noble of me. I am just lucky this worked out.

I knew that the way I would make a difference in this world was through small business—by selling people a product that they needed to solve a problem. And through my businesses, I would establish jobs for people so they could support their families. I would never feel the passion to help others by volunteering in a soup kitchen, but I could make my contribution to the world in this way.

I was very happy to discover this because I always felt guilty about not doing more volunteerism at social-service agencies. My parents had taught me to help others less fortunate than we were. After 20 years in business, I realize that we can all contribute to the world in different ways. I make my contribution through small business.

At my last company, I remember one of my employees became particularly ill and was in the hospital for months. I visited her there when she was feeling better. All she could do was thank me for being a part of our company. We had continued to pay her while she was in the hospital. She had never had health insurance or other benefits before coming to our company. She felt that without the company's support, she would have surely died and her family would have gone hungry.

This was one of the good days of being an entrepreneur.

My Business Is My Contribution

SO, WHERE DO I SIGN UP?

So what's the litmus test? How do you know if you have the passion that can sustain you through all the ups and downs of running a business? Some readers would want me to give a multiple-choice "passion test" at this point to determine whether they have what it takes. They would want ten questions to answer and then check their scores on the next page to see if they are good fits.

Sorry, there isn't one.

You will not really be able to answer the passion question until you are faced with choices. We can imagine all types of make-believe scenarios to ask the prospective entrepreneur, but the true answer about what you will do only comes at the point that you face the situation. I'm not sure that anything can prepare you for this.

I suggest, however, that you think about other circumstances in your life where you have bounced back from setbacks or have been able to focus on a new goal after a particular victory. During those times, what kept you going forward and what did you hold on to to steady yourself? Are you able to solve new problems as they arise and continue your momentum forward? If you can answer these questions, you will be close to locating your passion and your drive.

K *ay* K *oplovitz*

Kay Koplovitz says that as long as she can remember she wanted to run a television network. She started her career at a station in Milwaukee, where she learned the ropes. And she realized quickly that her inner vision of herself as a network president was not aligned with how others viewed her.

"I knew the people there did not look at this fresh-faced, 22-year-old woman and say she is going to be the next manager of our station, the next president of our company," she says. "God knows what I wanted to be was the president of NBC."

Koplovitz knew her passion early on, and throughout her life she has felt the rewards of her achievements at a very deep level.

"Psychic compensation is about the psychology of me," she says. "It is who we are, the essence of what drives the individual, how you feel about yourself. It goes to your core of who you are. We all know when we feel good about something we did, or when we don't particularly want to do what we are doing but we are doing it because we have to or because it is expected of us.

"[Passion] is something entirely different because we truly want to do it. I believe that people are most successful at what they want to truly do.

"I was speaking at the University of Vancouver about being an entrepreneur," she says, "and I was talking about the challenge and then how I suddenly got successful.

"After class this Chinese student came to me and asked, 'How do you know what's the right idea? I get ideas and then I get afraid.'

"I said 'That's not so unusual a thing for an entrepreneur.' It's daunting and people often have concerns and challenges, and it can be difficult. But I tell you what, one of these days you will get an idea that you really love, and you won't be afraid. And then you'll know for you that is the right idea."

Fighting back from the bottom of the well made me realize that my passions in life were my family and the contributions to this world I was making through my business.

Find Something You Can Hang On To

"What gets me really excited is that I could be creating a tool for social change. I am happy to do something that guides people through a process where they can find a more fulfilling and deeper commitment in their lives."

Alison Doree

ONLY EXPERIENCE TEACHES YOU

We all hear this so often, but the truth is that you need to go through something to truly learn it. Reading or being told about it is not a substitute. You can't learn skiing by watching videos. They might help but you still need to find a place with snow, put your skis on, and thrust yourself down the mountain. You need to experience the ups and downs. Forget it right now. There is no way to avoid the mistakes. You will fall and fail. Just learn from them and ride them out. I am a believer that not every bad thing that happens in business has something to teach us. Sometimes it's just a bad break and just stinks, and you need to wait until the next opportunity shows itself. But, at the very least, every experience makes you eliminate the possibility of making that same mistake more than one time. As an entrepreneur, eliminating what does not work can be as important as finding what does work. As Matt McCall at DFJ Portage Ventures says, the key to any start-up business is to fail with as many ideas as quickly as possible with as little money as possible.

A good example of this is Sean Lundgren, who started Smeetch.com in 1999 with a partner selling DVDs and videos over the Internet. As luck would have it, they were chosen as a featured store under Yahoo! Shopping. With only a few employees and a virtual company that shipped directly from distributors, sales and profit skyrocketed even though margins were tight. Sean had never taken any outside capital and never expanded beyond his means. In 2001, Yahoo! decided to raise its fee for being a part of its shopping network from 2 percent to 4 percent. In August 2001, Sean and his partner became scared that Yahoo! would eventually eat into all their profits in this narrow-margin business. They decided to contract with a development firm to create a Web site and order-processing system outside of Yahoo!. They wanted to go after the AOL shopping network as well. Smeetch migrated to its new Web site just before the holiday season of 2001. When January 2002 rolled around, Sean discovered an ugly surprise. Their new order-processing system had double- and sometimes triple-shipped all the customer orders directly from the distributors. Furthermore, the cash from the credit-card transactions was not going into their bank account. Someone else was taking their money! This amounted to a $160,000 loss and wiped them out. Sean's partner left him because he had not personally guaranteed the debts like Sean had. The development company that had launched their new site went bankrupt. Sean never saw what hit him. He was left alone to either surrender to bankruptcy or try to rebuild his company. Over the years, Sean has worked hard to rebuild his business alone and repay his debts.

In February 2003, the company finally became profitable again after a long struggle. However, a technical glitch on Yahoo! Shopping removed Smeetch from the site for almost a month. The company, in such a tenuous state, could not withstand the loss of an entire month's sales. In May 2003, Sean closed the doors of Smeetch and is currently filing for business and personal bankruptcy.

Sean learned that growing your company by changing your business model has risks. Changing the internal systems on how you perform something like process your orders is not always good. Technical problems can undermine your business. Partners don't always stay with you during bad times. And business can go from good to bad in a hurry. You could not have told Sean about this before all this happened to him. He had to experience it himself.

The Lessons Are Harder Than You Can Imagine

LOOK. LISTEN. LEARN

The best you can do is listen to all the advice around you. Listen to your customers. Listen to your business partners and vendors. Talk to your mentors. Then listen to your own successes and failures and blaze your own path.

The path you follow will be different than what you imagined. When I started my first business, I thought my path would be linear. I thought it would be similar to my professional career. I thought every year would get better. My mother had always instilled this hope in me. In my first business, I believed I would get a customer, then two, then three, and so on. I thought the company would build from just me and my partner to a few employees. Then we would grow so much that we would have to get a bigger office space. Soon, we would have hundreds of employees at offices all over the country. In this whole scenario, I had never planned to go out of business like we did less than a year later.

Think differently of the journey you will take in starting and running a company. Understand that your business is like driving a car on a mountainous winding road. You are constantly in motion forward and driving to what you think is higher. However, you are constantly banging and bouncing into the guardrails as you climb the mountain. Don't worry about the dents in your car. They don't need to be repaired. Think of them as medals of honor and scars of the battle. Focus on not crashing through one of the guardrails. Focus on staying on the road and not going off the side of the mountain into a ditch you are unable to climb out of.

Pay Attention to Everything

YOU'VE GOT COMPANY!

The good news is that if you feel the draw of passion to start a business and the fear of uncertainty, you are not alone. So many of us have been there before, making the same mistakes you have made or are about to make. I can only offer these lessons because I have made all these mistakes even though others had warned me. It's a kind of oral tradition and responsibility that entrepreneurs have for each other. This is also part of the entrepreneur's safety net. It is all around you. It is everyone who has gone through starting a business before, those who are in a business, or those contemplating starting a business. You will find a lot of good company in your fellow travelers.

This is where a business mentor comes in handy. If you do not have one, get one. She can be your unofficial therapist or your unwed partner in your business journey. She should be someone who has run her own business and felt your pain. There is nothing that can be substituted for having the opportunity to vent or talk things through with a person who is not involved in your business every day or who does not have it "all on the line" like you do. It will help vaporize your isolation and support you when you need it most.

There are only a few important qualities a mentor must possess. Primarily, she must be able to listen to you. After 15 years of personal and group therapy, I realized that what I was mostly paying for was the right to have someone listen to me. It was worth it! The process of articulating your thoughts from your head to your mouth for others to hear as a sounding board can help a lot. Many times, this is all you need.

Mentors should also be nonjudgmental. Your mentor should be someone who communicates in a way that will not make you feel stupid no matter what you say. The environment surrounding any conversation with a mentor should also feel safe. You should be able to say anything in confidence and know that it goes no further than the two of you.

Finally, you must mutually respect each other. Forget about older and wiser. Do you respect her point of view? Is she truly interested in your definition of personal and business success? You may not agree with her point of view, but do you trust her?

Like a mentor, I am warning you about the mistakes you have made or will make. But unlike a mentor, I will not tell you to avoid most types of warnings. Instead, I advise you to be aware, listen, and learn. I say, "Go ahead and make those mistakes." Then tell your story and remember what you learned. Try not to make the same mistake more than twice because then it becomes silly and wasteful.

Behind every financially successful entrepreneur are long stories of mistakes, failures, and hardships. You don't get to your goal without getting scars on your back. Rarely does a football player score a touchdown by going into the end zone untouched by an opponent. All financially successful entrepreneurs who are truly honest with themselves admit the hard times they went through to get to their pots of gold. They talk about how the mistakes almost cost them their businesses and how a crisis in confidence almost made them give up.

Many times in my last business as I traveled to work, I thought it would be more freeing to give up then to continue. Somehow, though, with encouragement from my partner, we always found a way out or, better said, a way through. Sometimes perseverance is enough.

You Are Not Alone. Bank on It

A True Tale
RANDY KOMISAR
Passion from Drive Leaves Bliss Behind

Randy Komisar sustains himself through passion, passion in his everyday life, passion in his everyday coaching of entrepreneurs, and passion in his everyday teaching of entrepreneurship students at Stanford.

A practicing Zen Buddhist, Komisar integrates his life and his work with a powerful core belief: Time is short. Don't squander any of it. Invest your time in only those things that are important. Because of this, he strives to make passion his constant companion.

Komisar says he recognized passion at the moment he lost it.

Komisar was CEO of LucasArts Entertainment when he was recruited to be CEO of Crystal Dynamics, a video-game company. He took the position because of the autonomy and the opportunity to make his mark. But most of all, Komisar took the job because he was drawn to the possibilities of interactive storytelling through new technology. He saw gaming as an entrance into that nascent world he felt so passionate about.

At Lucas he had found his work new and interesting and experimental, but the Crystal experience was falling short.

"While at Lucas I was full," he says. "But at Crystal at the end of the day, I felt exhausted. I was perplexed by the difference, until one day I was in a limo with a friend who was producing the sort of interactive work that I admired. She was floundering in the game business, but she was pushing the envelope of the new art form. 'You are in the fucking game business,' she declared."

After trying to justify himself, Komisar realized she was right. His new job was to run a company that invented games where fictional characters blew each other up. Within a month he was no longer in the game business, he had moved on.

"Deferring my passion in the hopes that success at something else, for example, making video games, would eventually allow me to reengage that passion simply doesn't work for me," Komisar says. Because then, Komisar has chosen full engagement. He says this was a difficult path to choose.

We tend to follow a certain sequence in life, Komisar says. "First, do what we must. Second, do what you want." We exist from day-to-day in a state of "deferred life."

"At Crystal, I was completely on drive and off passion," he says. "Since Crystal, I have thought a lot about passion. As a young man, I found myself highly driven. As I have gotten older I have questioned the difference between drive and passion.

"Every once in awhile I would find someone who was truly engaged," he says. "They seemed to have the satisfaction and contentment of being truly merged with what they were doing.

"I began to look at that condition and try to understand the difference between that and drive," he says. "I was watching hardworking, smart people, driving themselves to exhaustion.

"I simplified my life and ambitions," he says, "and I began to look at passion as an expression of who I was.

"Passion pulls you forward," he says. "There is no way to avoid it. You have to go there. It is the siren's call. It is the sense of getting up every morning to do what you want to do.

"Drive consumes energy," he says. "You've got to get up and push. Whereas passion creates energy because it fully engages body and soul. Even though activities appear just as exhausting, people [operating from passion] come back replenished.

"Clearly that is what I wanted to create in my life," he says.

His study of passion has grown through his work teaching entrepreneurship students at Stanford University.

"Most of these kids come to me with this confused look on their faces," Komisar says. "'Please tell me what my passion is?' They are full of passions. They want to find the one passion that will guide them through their entire lives.

"I think that people have many passions," he says. "What paralyzes them is when they try to think about that one passion, and their life's passion.

"What I have come to understand is that we have a rich spectrum of passions," he says. "Why should we feel that one passion would guide us through our entire life?

"There is this serial monogamy with passion," he says. "A passion is constantly reenergizing you and bringing you to that next level of excitement and engagement in the world. It opens new doors, leads to new choices, and unlocks new passions in the process.

"I try to get my students to consider all their passions," he says, "starting with the ones that they engage with where they are today. I also want them to realize that their lives will be this savory stew of passions. Some of them will be coexistent, others have not yet emerged.

"I want them to realize that those passions might change over time," he says. "From a career standpoint, you might find yourself working in a commercial enterprise, a nonprofit, and then becoming a writer.

"It is hard for 22-year-olds who have spent their lives in school to see this," he says. "What they see is just another set of hurdles, they don't have a sense of that horizon of opportunities that will be available to them for the next 50 to 60 years."

In his book, *The Monk and the Riddle,* Komisar asks the question: "What would you do for the rest of your life?" He says in a world of multiple passions that question still holds true. Simply expand the context:

"If this is the last moment of your life, you must be fully engaged with those things that you are truly passionate about," he says. "It doesn't mean that tomorrow you won't wake up and find yourself with a new set of opportunities and a new way to engage a different passion. But in each moment be sure your passion is engaged as if it were the last moment of your life.

"The world is dynamic," he says. "You must be fully engaged with those things that you are doing right now. Doing each fully. Doing each passionately."

The passion conversation takes a different shape and form when it's with a middle-aged man or woman who has come away from the first part of his or her life experience with some success but nevertheless discontentment.

"It becomes this process of realizing what you can and can't afford," Komisar says. "Lots of people don't understand what is required to maintain the lifestyle that is suitable and that allows them the freedom to pursue their passion. They feel they have to have this kind of house; the kids have to go to these kinds of schools. I encourage them to examine every one of those assumptions and begin to identify the kernel of truth to whittle them down and simplify.

"You can get rid of some of these processes and biases that hold you back," he says. "You can become more realistic about what is necessary. And in doing so your engagement with passion increases as your freedom to pursue it increases; not with the attainment of more but with the need for less."

Komisar says that there are definitely times in life when we are more open to considering our passions and that gender differences do exist, too.

"Women are more open-minded," he says. "They are more empowered to creatively engage their passions because they are disadvantaged in pursuing conventional paths. Women generally undertake this quest much better than men do, in part, because women have commonly been excluded from men's traditional opportunities.

"The now almost cliché dilemma of being the supermom is about balancing two passions. Most women want to be both satisfied moms and successful professionals because they have passion for both," Komisar says. "Women get it.

"Men adhere to other people's expectations very easily," he says. Their whole identity often amounts to a single thing, a successful career. They suffer from one dimensionality. When I discuss drive versus passion I am often challenged by young, well-educated white men. They have a million different reasons why [passion] won't work. Their life is a set of hurdles, a racecourse for blind ambition. The wealth of conventional opportunities available to them does not encourage them to take a risk on engaging their passions. Their social empowerment limits their willingness to create a truly passionate life.

"In middle age, people seem to open up to the possibility of living passionately again. And even the most successful men I know want to talk about these issues of success and satisfaction, drive and passion."

But, Komisar adds, passion should never be confused with bliss.

"Following your bliss is about attempting to maximize your pleasure at every turn," he says. "Following your bliss says 'Don't make me do that hard work. I don't want to make any sacrifices for my passions.'

"Following passion does not bring you pleasure all the time," he says. "Following passion can be very hard work—it is very engaging. It can be very intense.

"But passion is always engaging that part of you that is expressing yourself in the moment," he says. "Even though that something you are doing is not something that you love to be doing at that moment, it is still differentiated from drive or compulsion. There is deep satisfaction in engaging body and soul, even when the work is difficult.

"For me, life is much more fulfilling when my passion is engaged, when my passion is leading me. And now I am far more acutely aware when it is missing."

2

CONTROLLING THE ROLLER COASTER

You Can't Lose Something
You Never Had

IT'S YOUR UNIQUE WAY
ON THE HIGHWAY

Over the years, I have searched for the perfect formula for business success. Like most of us, I wanted to know the common traits shared by financially successful entrepreneurs. How do you actually build and run a successful business?

Most titles of business books make me angry because they say there are ten steps to business success. Amazon.com lists hundreds of these books. Why are there always ten steps? I'd think that with all the technology in our fast-paced world, those ten could have been narrowed down to five by now! These books sell well because we are always looking for *the* way to get there. Would-be entrepreneurs want to be told specifically the step-by-step approach. They want to shortcut the experience of truly figuring it out for themselves. Although a how-to book might give the reader some comfort because it gives him or her a direction, it ultimately fails because it describes a situation that is not easily transferable to the entrepreneur's situation. Regardless of what popular books say, there is no single way to achieve the personal success that you seek.

So, the good news is that there is no one way. Few things bind financially successful people together, and many paths will take you there. You can approach your business from many different angles and still arrive successfully.

The bad news is that there is no road map. You need to find your own way through your own experience and shape your own business. This is what you are signing up for when you start a business: responsibility for your own fate and the path you follow. Right or wrong, it is your decision.

Looking to place blame on others does not accomplish anything. The only right path for your business will be the one you take. The "buck" truly stops with you. This is what you told yourself you wanted, to be your own boss. Be careful of what you wish for because as an entrepreneur you will surely achieve this one!

Y*our* W*ay* I*s the* O*nly* W*ay*

"I raised $31 million in four weeks for Blue Meteor [Corporation]. They turned over $28 million to a 28-year-old. While I was in that mind if you had said failure or mistake, I could not handle it . . . because I couldn't acknowledge that I was making mistakes."

"You have to execute, you have to make the right decisions. But the planets have to be aligned. Success has things outside your control. Your failure is pure. You cannot take total credit for success. But you must take responsibility for failure."

David Weinstein

THERE IS NO ROAD MAP

When starting your business, you must blaze your own path. Zen Buddhists say that to be happy, you should live in accordance with your "own true nature." They say that life is filled with "10,000 joys and 10,000 sorrows."

To be happily successful in business, you must do the same thing: Listen to all that is offered to you, but integrate all that you hear into your own way. You truly can't be happily successful by simply replicating someone else's path. You will not get there. The best news about this is that because there is no road map, you can't get lost!

I am telling you about my path, not because I am particularly proud of it—although I am happy to have survived it. I am telling you so you will know that you are not alone. This will help during the difficult days to come in running your own business. In this case, men are allowed to ask for directions. But while others can guide you, the final decisions are yours. Let your experience speak to you and show you the way. Make a decision based on the imperfect information you have, and go with it. My advice has always been to make a decision, any decision. It is the one thing in your business you have true control over.

U se Your Own Internal Compass

> "I agree with President Dwight Eisenhower when he said: 'I have always found that plans are useless, but planning is indispensable.' Things rarely turn out the way the plan works, but the process of having thought through the alternatives and being able to deal with multiple scenarios and thinking broadly is indispensable."
>
> **Bob Okabe**

CONTROL FREAKS NEED NOT APPLY

I am not a traveler. I hate waves when I sail, and I hate turbulence when I fly. Maybe it's because, like most entrepreneurs, I like being in control. Most days, this is not the case when running a business. This was the hardest thing for me to understand when I first began. Many people start businesses so they can control their own destinies. We want to be our own bosses. We want to be the one sitting in the high-back black leather chair calling all the shots!

What an entrepreneur comes to realize is that control becomes more elusive as the business fills his or her life with even more variables. More people, more customers, more vendors, and more issues— all this on some days leads to no control at all. I wondered many times whether I was leading the company or whether the company was leading me.

As an entrepreneur, you must be able to accept business outcomes outside of your control. Period. This was very difficult for me to accept. I have had to learn to ride the business roller coaster and some days just accept the grinding bumps up and the steep slide down.

You can control the decisions you make for your business—that's it. Make decisions without getting paralyzed that you do not have enough information or that your decisions might be wrong. Make the decision with the information you have. Look and learn from the outcome and make another decision.

Your Company Has You By the Nose

"If you're brilliant, 15 percent to 20 percent of the risk is removed. If you work 24 hours per day, another 15 percent to 20 percent of the risk is removed. The remaining 60 percent to 70 percent of business risk will be completely out of your control."
—*The Monk and the Riddle*

Randy Komisar

CAN YOU HANDLE THE UPS AND DOWNS?

While you ride the roller coaster of good and bad times in running your business, it is important to remember the good times so you can survive the motion sickness. These good times are something you can hold on to. This is why I believe that trophies are so important in our society. We can place them on our desks or in our bookcases and look at them to remember that we were at the top of our game that day. I remember when I used to receive monetary awards and trophies from IBM, I always cherished and proudly displayed the trophy more than the money. I also tried to take part of the money to buy something that I could remember this honor with like a shirt.

Again, similar to the trophy, whenever I wore that shirt or played with that new racket, I could remember my achievement that day. The rest of the money would be spent on bills and would be long forgotten.

During tough times, I would go back to letters of praise, the trophy mementos, favorable newspaper articles, or journal writings to give me the lift I needed. I had experienced good times before, and I would experience them again. If you know that good times will return, this can sustain you when you are at the bottom of the roller coaster.

There is no solution here. Do what you must do on any roller coaster: Hold on and ride.

R*emember the* U*ps*

"There are no rules. You make them up on the fly. You drive it personally and the people around you drive it. There is no way to really understand what that is going to be like. You feel it. . . . It is something in your gut. You follow it blindly."

Jodi Turek

UNIVERSAL TRUTH #1: LUCK

After searching for the perfect formula for success, I found only two common elements: luck and timing.

The question is always asked as a choice: Would you rather be lucky or be good? I always give the same answer: lucky. In the business world, luck makes you good. If I am unlucky, then no matter what I do, it's very hard to be successful. I always look for luck. My father-in-law, Mike Cooper, had the right attitude when he told me, "Just play. Someone has to win the Lotto, why not me?"

One of my favorite quotes about luck is by Jean Cocteau, the French dramatist and movie director. He said, "We must believe in luck for how else can we explain the success of those we do not like."

Here's how luck plays an important role in your business. You get a call from a prospect you have been courting for a year saying that its current Web development firm just went out of business. Could you take over the $100,000 project they had just started? Were you lucky or good? Probably both since you stayed in touch with the prospect, so when they had a need, they called you. You put yourself in the right place at the right time. We don't typically sell people anything. Usually we put ourselves into the position so that when they are ready to buy, we are there for them to choose us.

Here's another example. You just closed a software development contract with a client for $250,000. It's the largest sale of your career. A month later, the Securities and Exchange Commission (SEC) indicts the client. The project is canceled, and months later, the company dissolves. Were you unlucky? Absolutely.

We all need to learn to accept business outcomes outside of our control. So what is an entrepreneur to do? Sit by the phone while fate and luck take their course? No, work hard to achieve your personal success. Celebrate the victories, and transition through the disappointments. And just in case, carry your lucky rabbit's foot wherever you go.

Keep the **R**abbit's **F**oot **H**andy

_____

UNIVERSAL TRUTH #2: TIMING

Here's an expression that is universally applicable to running a business: "Timing isn't everything, it's the only thing."

If it were not for the Internet bubble of the late 1990s, I may have never sold my last business. The company that bought us was looking for a quick way into the New Economy. Back then, we were all headed in that direction. They thought our company was a shortcut in. If we were trying to sell our company today, postbubble, I doubt it would be worth as much as it was worth then. Many companies were sold during this time for prices that seem ridiculous today.

An important part of being an entrepreneur is to be able to accept the role that serendipity plays in any business outcome. These "fortunate discoveries" can also provide a lift to your company. In my last business, 25 percent of our revenue came from a source we did not even consider until a customer suggested it to us. We discovered a major revenue stream by accident.

As an entrepreneur, welcome both Lady Luck and Father Fate in your business. They will fit well alongside your daily hard work.

Accept and **I**nvite the **U**nexpected

_____

A r i K a p l a n

Ari Kaplan saw a problem with baseball statistics, and who doesn't? The difference between Kaplan and other observers is that Kaplan set out to improve them.

"You know baseball statistics and inertia. You are always met with skepticism. It's been done this way for 100 years, why would we need to change?

"I had this idea of these new statistics for baseball, called Reliever Effectiveness. So at Caltech, I did a summer undergraduate research project (SURP) where I wrote a proposal, and I received funding from Caltech to investigate this baseball hypothesis.

"I gave a presentation to the Board of Trustees of CalTech. There was a guy on the board who raised his hand and said, 'Hi, I'm the owner of the Baltimore Orioles, I'd like to offer you a job.'

"It was one of my happiest days. I said, 'I accept. Please don't leave the room without my contact information.' I worked for the Orioles.

"Baseball is a very difficult community to break into, but once you get your foot in the door, if you do a good job word gets around."

IT'S HOW YOU HANDLE FAILURE

It is not a question of whether you will fail as an entrepreneur, it is simply a question of when and how. One key to being a happily successful entrepreneur is the way you handle failure.

An entrepreneur is defined by how he or she handles failure, not by how he or she handles success. In your business, you will unfortunately have more opportunities to bounce back from failure than to celebrate your victories. You will have wonderful days in your business that you will want to never end. The sun will shine on you the entire day, and it will seem that you have the golden touch. Customers, colleagues, friends, and family will call you Midas. These days you will wish that you lived in Yellowknife in the Northwest Territories of Canada where in the summertime the day never ends.

Unfortunately, eventually, the sun will set.

During these long periods of darkness seemingly nothing can go right. Now, you will know that you have moved to Barrow, Alaska, where the sun never rises in December. How do you handle yourself during those gloomy times? Do you immediately give up or can you find things inside yourself to drive you forward?

Failure is not a destination. It is only a point on your business journey. Consider it a rest stop if that helps you. A time and place to sit for a moment and evaluate what has happened and what you have achieved. Then get back in your dented car, start it up, and get going again.

Own and **H**onor **Y**our **F**ailures

"When things go very well you learn nothing. When you teach entrepreneurship all you teach is business failure."

Mohnish Pabrai

FAILURE IS NOT PERSONAL

While a start-up business is personal, you are not the business. If the business does fail, it does not mean that you are a failure. Many factors outside your control can lead to that outcome. But don't blame others or blame your helpless circumstances. Learn what you can about your failure, feel sorry for a few weeks, wallow well in it, if that helps you. Then move on.

This is an especially difficult concept for men, whose self-worth traditionally is tied to the financial success they achieve for themselves and their family. After all, we are the hunters! Men "kill the food" and bring it back to their family. This has been the tradition for hundreds of thousands of years. I feel the same responsibility today. But what men hunt today is not buffalo, but a livelihood. We hunt for money so we can bring our families food and shelter, and the other things we want in life. Much of society sees us as the economic engine for our families. Men provide, and woman care for the family while the men are out. Failing financially is especially difficult for men because society judges us by what we have provided for our families. When so much of financial success has to do with luck and timing, this outcome seems especially cruel.

It can be equally difficult for women who have chosen career over family and have decided to be hunters, too. Many women choose to work through their children's early years or perhaps to forgo having children altogether to pursue a career. Their self-worth is now totally tied up in their financial success. Any failure can be equally devastating.

So how do you deal with a blow to your self-worth in the face of failure? Know that you did everything you could to succeed. Know that through hard work, you and your family may not get rich but just as surely, you will never go hungry. Know that you are not a failure; know instead that a series of events has occurred. It's only a point in time, and it will pass.

Financial Success Is Not Always within Your Control

"People who are great at chess have the ability to focus three to seven moves ahead, and even more," he says, "and they understand the likely permutations. It's great for them, because they love that."

"After a while, I found it boring," he says. "It's like sitting there and knowing how the movie's going to end. . . . The range of outcomes is relatively narrow."

"Running a business is not chess."

Bob Okabe

FAILURE IS THE GREAT TEACHER

Failure gives you humility, which is an important quality for any entrepreneur and happily successful person. I didn't learn to be humble by getting awards at IBM or wearing Hugo Boss suits at Whittman-Hart. I learned to be humble by failing.

When I left IBM in the late 1980s, one of my mentors was a long-time IBM manager, Tom Liebtag. He told me that I was a pretty good businessperson. He also told me that I would be really good when I had failed more. IBM had trained me in success, but it did not tolerate failure. At the time, I felt he said this to me because he was jealous that I had found a great new job, and that I was going to make a lot more money than he made. At the time, I did not realize that he was foretelling the next five years of my professional life.

Tom was right. After I was fired from Whittman-Hart, and kicked out of my business with two other partners, I tasted failure. At times, I wanted to limp back to IBM and try to get my old job back. I had learned the important entrepreneurial skill of being humble.

Along with being focused and watching your cash flow, humility is the next most important skill you need to learn. While running your own business, you do not have a corporate logo to hide behind or a long history of business relationships to protect you.

Humility keeps you sharp on your business edge. Things are fragile and can change very quickly. The expression is true: "You meet the same people on the way up as you do on the way down." I have passed the same people as I have traveled in both directions.

Humility makes you perform better as a businessperson. You appreciate your gains and accept your failures. You value the contributions of others. You realize that although you may be riding high today, tomorrow might bring a different experience. Humble people can face the next day with excitement and anticipation regardless of the outcome.

The sooner you learn this lesson, the better off you will be. You will learn to be thankful for what you are able to achieve.

L e a r n   t h e   S *k i l l   o f*   H *u m i l i t y*

"Starting a company is all about learning from your successes and failures. You figuratively and literally live paycheck to paycheck, because you're selling, you're closing, you're delivering, you're working from project to project, trying to build a loyal customer base, but there's clearly a period of time at the beginning when you're trying to build your brand and build your reputation when there's very little that you can control."

"Without humility, you don't listen. I talk a lot about how important dialogue is, not only among ourselves, but with our customers. A person without humility reverts to monologue: I'm going to tell you what to do; or this is the way it should be. Dialogue is when you listen, and when you listen, you learn; and when you learn, you really understand what a customer values. When you finally understand what a customer values, then you can, in turn, create the solution to provide that value."

David Ormesher

WHAT HUMILITY TEACHES YOU

I succeeded for almost a decade at IBM. I was promoted almost every year and won many awards. I began to take it for granted and feel "entitled" to my success. I thought that the world had "destined" me for something special. But I did not really feel like a winner until years later when I had a successful business after being fired from other jobs and going out of business on previous attempts. I could only cherish my victory after I had been humbled by losses. You can't really smile broadly until you know what it's like to frown for a very long time.

At IBM, I did not realize that my success was largely attributable to my being able to successfully adapt to the artificial system that a large corporation like IBM can set up and maintain from within. Promotions and awards were distributed. I worked hard, and I did get some of them. This was not recognition of my achievement from the market, rather it was recognition from members of a hierarchical management team. This is neither good nor bad, it is just the way large corporations work.

When I sold products for IBM in the 1980s, My phone calls were returned because I was calling from the highly respected company called IBM. It was a free ticket to get in to see any prospect. As the expression goes, "No one ever got fired for choosing to buy from IBM." The products and services I offered were a safe choice for any customer.

But when you have your own business, you no longer can personally hide behind the logo of a large corporation. As an entrepreneur you are going out into the market as the emperor with no clothes. You are naked and vulnerable to the business world. Your products and services are not safe choices anymore. In contrast, you represent risk and an unknown outcome.

I remember my experience with some customers and business partners who did not return my calls after I left IBM. Even though I was selling a service that could solve a problem they had, they did not know this company, "Whittman-Hart," and forgot about me. This was a hard adjustment and realization. My contacts at IBM, whom I had depended on, had evaporated.

In the end, humility also teaches you that it's OK to be an emperor with no clothes while you are running your own business. Be free, and be proud of it. You have less to lose. Accept that you have no clothes and find customers who will do business with you even while you are still naked.

C *elebrate* B *eing* N *aked*

FORGET VINCE LOMBARDI. DO YOU KNOW WHEN TO GIVE UP?

As in the game of poker, how do you know when to "hold 'em and when to fold 'em"? In any given business venture, how do you know when it is time to give up and go out of business?

Yes, it is OK to go out of business.

Most businesses don't succeed. Like all things in our world, every business has its own life cycle. There are no business prizes given out for martyrdom (except maybe in my Jewish family). Sometimes it is better to quit, take a break, or start over.

Vince Lombardi, Green Bay Packers coach, said that "winners never quit and quitters never win." Growing up, I heard my dad repeat this many times. It is only after being in the business world for more than 20 years that I realize that it's simply not true; it's not that winners never quit, they know when to quit and how to quit. Vince Lombardi also said that, "the harder you work, the harder it is to surrender." I agree that many times it is a lot harder to quit whatever adventure you are involved in than it is to keep going.

I admire these people who know when to get out. They had a vision of doing something, but when they could not make it work, they called it quits and moved on to something else. This is harder to do in practice than on paper. In business, you wait because you always think that the next prospect, or the next customer, or the next consultant will make the difference and propel your business. It rarely happens this way. Most of the time, we spend too long going down the same path, doing the same thing and hoping for it to change.

I remember in 1997, I was riding my bike to work when things were going particularly bad in my business. I remember wanting to call it quits. I felt it was just too hard to make it work. The realization that day that I could close it down and walk away was strangely freeing. It gave me a choice. We eventually did stick it out and turn the business around.

Manish Patel describes having the same feeling of freedom with Where2GetIt: "The minute I figured out that this wasn't something I was going to do forever, and there was something better out there, that's really when my attitude started changing," he says. "At that point you know the business is failing, you can face reality, you can shut it down. If the business needs something that you can't provide, then your ego doesn't get in the way."

"What's your walkaway point?" Patel asks. "What's the point when you're going to say, enough is enough and I'm going to just shut it down, shut my business. Some people let the business go on too long, and sometimes that is the cause of their own failure, their family's failure, because they just don't know when to walk away. Lucky for me I learned that just in the nick of time, that I could have a walkaway point."

How do you know to stay the course with a business or close it? First, if you and the business continue to fall deeper into debt on a monthly basis then shut down. It is similar to what Will Rogers said: "If you find yourself in a hole, the first thing to do is stop diggin'." Second, if you have lost the passion for the business or if you no longer like the people you are working with, it is time to close the doors.

If this is your choice, remember you are not alone. There is no shame in surrender. In fact, surrender offers you new possibilities and a fresh start. Many businesses that start out one way end up to be completely different businesses.

Lombardi Also Said, "It's Not Whether You Get Knocked Down, It's Whether You Get Up"

CROSSING FORBIDDEN LINES

I started my first business after I had read an idealistic book written by Paul Hawken called *Growing Your Business*. My first business was filled with hopes, dreams, and fantasies of a perfect culture. After this business died a year later, I was more realistic. The decisions I'd made had crossed lines I had never known existed.

When we started my last business, my partner and I had a celebratory dinner with our spouses to kick it off. We talked about how great it would be, and about how we would remain ethical faced with all choices. We discussed different scenarios and situations. I distinctly remember our answers from that evening. We detailed what we would do and what we would not do. In the next five years, I stepped over and back, and over and back that gray line repeatedly. My actual responses to situations as they arose bore little resemblance to what we had said that evening.

There is a part of me that always looks for a shortcut. Some days I pretend that rules do not apply to me. Unfortunately, I have always admired something about P. T. Barnum who could always attract paying customers to his sideshow carnivals.

If you have these types of days, your reasoning might go something like this. You see an opportunity to strike out on your own where you can make a lot of money. You start by congratulating yourself that this brilliant plan is perfectly legal and maybe even ethical. You reason that no one will get hurt. You may even be right.

But somewhere along the way things begin to go wrong or you get greedy.

The equation changes and you become desperate. You cross the gray legal and ethical lines once too often and permanently begin pursuing financial gain for its own sake regardless of how others may lose in the process. Your methods become overly aggressive, flamboyant, and devious. You stop wanting to build anything or deliver solutions to your customers. You only want to make money for yourself regardless of the cost to others. Then the worst thing happens: Everyone else in your company follows your "example." Your goals become further warped and your reasoning is out of control.

At this point, I suggest you step back to remember that desperate people do desperate things. After 20 years in business, I still have to remind myself of this. Think about whether the ends really justify the means. Sooner or later, these businesses always come crashing down.

Sometimes You Can't Get Back

ETHICAL DECISIONS ARE NOT EASY

What I learned was that the decisions you make in your business are not black-and-white. They are shades of gray. You will find yourself stepping over your personal line not realizing that you are there until it's very late. You will try to convince yourself that the ends do justify the means. And you will realize that you can't anticipate what you will do until you find yourself in the position of having to make a choice.

I did many things to keep my business growing that I am not necessarily proud of in hindsight, but I thought at the time that the means justified the ends. In my last business, when we had just started, I remember when our first customer wanted to visit to check us out. We had no employees and no furniture in our office. We thought this would hurt our chances of landing our first customer. So a few days before our customer came to visit, we purchased a lot of furniture on a credit card with a 30-day return guarantee. We had our computers dial our phone system to make it seem like we were a busy company receiving a lot of calls. I also "hired" a few good friends for the day to make it seem like we had at least a few employees. It worked out well for we landed the customer as a large client. After we sent all the furniture back we faced another problem. The customer wanted to come back a month later to visit us again!

Three years later, we were bidding for a customer project that would add 20 percent to our revenue growth. They wanted to come visit our warehouse to see if we were large and efficient enough to handle their capacity. I remember that I instructed our warehouse staff to assemble empty boxes and label them as product and put them on our bare shelves. This was to make it seem like we had more product in our warehouse than we actually had. They were impressed for we got the business!

I justified both of these situations because I wanted the prospects to give us a chance. Many people don't want to work with small companies that do not have a track record of success. I knew we could do a good job for them. Right or wrong, I just had to dress up that perception a bit. Through excellent results, we managed to keep both of these customers for a long time.

By far the most difficult ethical dilemma I faced was when we received a $58,000 check from a customer that owed us only $950. This was a multibillion-dollar Fortune 500 company, and the check came to us at a time when cash flow was particularly tight. We were having trouble meeting payroll and our obligations to our vendors. Depositing this money in our bank account would smooth out our cash flow and enable the business to get to the next more profitable quarter. I was faced with three choices. I could send the check back immediately to the Fortune 500 company with a letter saying that they had made a mistake and please send me the $950 they owed our company. Alternatively, I could deposit the check, credit the $58,000 toward their $950, and leave a credit balance of $57,050. I would then wait for them to come "find" the money. Their credit balance would leave us with plenty of cash to meet our other current obligations. The Fortune 500 company would unknowingly be giving us a loan. I struggled with what was the best ethical decision and what was the best business decision.

What I did was deposit the check in our account and apply the $58,000 toward their balance. We called them up and told them that they had a $57,050 credit balance with us. What did they want us to do with it? Would they be placing a large order with us in the near future? They thanked us for calling and said they would get back with instructions. It took them six months before they asked for their money back. Their cash was important to the survival of our company.

It is important to remember that your business code of ethics gets built incrementally over time with everyday decisions. There are typically few big things that set a course for a lifetime. Each small decision you make as you go back and forth over this "thick gray line" builds the kind of businessperson you are and the kind of company you are a part of. You need to realize that most of these decisions produce both good and bad results.

As Red Clark, CEO of Metalforming Controls, says: "When I find myself offtrack, it is rarely because I made a conscious decision to do something dishonest or marginally honest, rather it has been caused by a series of spur-of-the-moment decisions that gradually move you in a wrong direction. Living ethically is an ongoing effort."

Although I am not proud of every decision I have made, I accept responsibility for making each one of them. I learn from what I did right and wrong in each situation. I hope this will help every day I struggle with my next one. Having your own personal struggle will help you, too.

Watch Your Step

EVEN YOUR SUCCESSES CAN
ALMOST KILL YOU

Even if you find the gold at the end of the rainbow, and you sell your business, you are still riding the roller coaster. Most business acquisitions get called off at least once. The sale of my last business was called off twice. Like a Buddhist monk, I died and was reborn several times.

My partner and I were approached in December 1998 by a larger private company that wanted to buy our business. This was during the Internet bubble, and we saw an opportunity to cash out. Over the next four months, we were courted by this company. We finally received an offer that we accepted. Months of due diligence followed where they found flaws in our business that I did not even know existed. At that moment, I realized that the highest price an owner will ever get for his business is what the term sheet says. The final purchase price will always be lower. The deal was called off. One of the main partners at the acquiring company was against it. This was equally difficult for me because I had already mentally sold the business and moved on in my own mind.

I remember during this time bicycling to work and wanting to just give away the business and move on. I was emotionally and physically spent over this process. We kept talking to them. The deal was renegotiated at a lower price. The deal was back on. Months later, the sale was completed. I was exhausted. My partner and I "celebrated" the sale of the company by participating in an all-night bike ride in Chicago. But we were celebrating our survival, not really the sale of our business.

Celebrate **S**urviving

THE WORST THEY CAN DO IS EAT YOU

The difficulties of running a start-up business are all around. The ups and downs test your passion and resolve. Obstacles spring from your competition, your partners, your family, and yourself. I had days that were so dark that I thought I would never last.

During these difficult times, my best friend, Zane, who is an attorney, would say to me: "The worst they can do is eat you, and that's illegal." He turned the world on its head for me. I had never thought of it that way.

Somehow, imagining that unlikely scenario helped. When it feels like you can't get any lower, thinking absurdly provides you with just enough hope to pull yourself up and move on to another, better day. Many times, just enough hope gets you through. Just knowing that your business survived today is an accomplishment in itself.

When you can go no lower, it is freeing. You have nothing to lose. If the worst they could do is eat me, and the "law" would protect me from that, then I still had a choice. I could still take a chance to battle back and turn the business around. Or I could quit, close it down, file for bankruptcy, and fight another day. Always having a choice will relieve you from a lot of pressure. Any business situation has alternatives because they can do a lot to you at the end of the day, except they cannot eat you!

B*on* A*ppétit!*

A T*rue* T*ale*
MANISH PATEL *Almost Losing Yourself*

In 1997, Manish Patel seized the opportunity he had been waiting for all his life: He started his own business. In what appeared to be a fortuitous alignment of events, Patel formed a partnership with a more experienced entrepreneur to start Where2getit, which offers location-based Web and marketing services and operates in the same Internet space as Mapquest.

Patel's former boss had introduced him to his new partner, and they moved ahead with the business after drafting a brief partnership agreement. Starry-eyed at the allure of finally being involved with a start-up, Patel put his back into creating the core services of the business.

It wasn't too long before Patel could sense that the partnership wasn't exactly even. He and his partner hadn't really known each other before the business started, and it wasn't too long before they were having communication problems.

When there was a disagreement, the conversation would stop. By its nature the relationship had to be close, but it wasn't. And Patel began to sense that the workload was unequal.

At one point, "We actually stood up an yelled at each other," Patel says. "As long as I was willing to be a lackey things were OK. The minute I started to stand up a little bit, then the specter started to rear its head."

In 1998—at the height of the Internet bubble—Patel's partner decided she wanted to sell the business. Patel wanted to build it to last. This was the first in a series of fundamental disagreements about the direction of the business, and Patel found that the partnership agreement did not offer any support for resolving these issues.

When the *Chicago Sun-Times* ran an article on the company in November 2001, the article stated that Patel was president, CEO, and chairman. But according to the partnership agreement, Patel was chairman and chief operating officer, not CEO, which was his partner's title. That's when the war began in earnest.

Patel's partner brought in the attorneys. They charged Patel with systematically expensing costs to the company that were not the company's, alleging something that sounded suspiciously like stealing. Patel and his partner were fighting the details via e-mail. As the threats volleyed back and forth, Patel dug in, hired lawyers, and started to spend what would eventually amount to $15,000 in legal fees.

The Where2GetIt partners were warring, the business was flat-lining. But oddly, Patel found himself comfortable in the painful rut.

"You just become numb to the environment," he says.

Patel felt the same way day in and day out. Days became undistinguishable, dreary, and with a steady crushing level of stress.

"On one hand, you have the fear of the unknown," he says. "And on the other hand, you have a situation you know, and even though it's a situation you don't necessarily want to be in, the sense of comfort, I guess, is in what you know.

"You don't trust the person across the table from you," he says. "You don't know what will happen when you are not there."

Patel felt that he was banging his head against a wall with no resolution. Finally, he decided to step back and take some time off to reflect, to read and to better understand his situation. He decided that he needed to find help for himself and his business because he couldn't go on the way it had been any longer. He started talking to anybody who would listen about his situation. He started asking for help.

That's when a series of events created the tipping point for change in his business.

In July 2002, Patel was flying from Chicago to Los Angeles and through a series of mishaps wound up sitting next to a stranger on the plane who was wearing a very similar jacket. They struck up a conversation that lasted the duration of the flight.

"We spoke about getting away from toxic people. About how to honor your spouse. About the fact that kids pass through your life and you're lucky to have them in your presence," he says.

"The biggest thing I still remember," Patel says, " is that your spouse could have married any number of people, yet they chose to marry you, and that you should feel lucky in their presence."

Patel felt that he had made himself open to the universe during the period from April through July and that people—like this man—were coming to aid him. His colleague on the plane had given him some basic tenets to hold on to that apply everywhere in every walk of life, the first being to get rid of toxic people.

"What happens is that the toxicity just builds on itself," Patel says. "It's a downward spiral, and you really can't get out of it; because the more you're in it, it's like this whirlpool. It will just draw you down, financially and emotionally. It's this whirlpool draining everything out of your life.

"The more that you have of it, the faster the thing spins, and the faster it spins out of control."

At the end of the day, what Patel came to understand was that he had to change the status quo to make a difference in the situation. He began to think of the business as a chair that he was stuck to. He hated sitting in it, but he was afraid to leave it fearing someone else would take it.

"One of the biggest things that I remember [learning] was 'the principle of' movement. You just have to move, just keep moving, moving, moving. Movement is the key in life and in business. Good or bad, make a decision. Don't just sit there," Patel says. "If you have to shut it down, then shut it down.

"You have to face what's on the other side," Patel says. "In general, we were in a rotten situation. There was a lot of venom. . . . There was a lot of ego, a lot of greed, and a lot of me wanting to hold on to something."

Patel says that when he started thinking that he could walk away, things began to change.

"Everything changed the day I started acting differently," Patel says. "Part of the change was to remove attachment to the business and attachment to the chair. When I started to let go, things started to happen.

"The minute I started letting go, it came back to me tenfold," he says.

"'Let go'" in the sense of mentally letting go of the business, mentally saying that I'm no longer attached to the business. Everything is temporary, even relationships," he says. "And I felt for the longest time that this was something I was going to do forever."

Patel looked at who was the most miserable in the situation. And he saw himself, sitting and suffering. He began to understand that "the bold move is to know when to hold and know when to fold."

Patel says that when he put the two together—changing the status quo and getting rid of toxic people—and then added the critical ingredient—acting on it—he had built a foundation for true change. He knew that he would be in a better spot no matter what happened to the business.

"It's almost like being an alcoholic," Patel says. "You have to first acknowledge that you have a problem, which I did in April, and that I needed help. I went about finding people, mentors, like the guy on the plane, to people who actually can give you some real-life advice."

But "even going through all that, you still had to make the change yourself," Patel says. "I think it's part of just that whole process. You have to be open to it and you can't force it; it's just going to have to happen."

In terms of the partner situation, Patel now understands the importance of having a tiebreaker vote and also to have people on the outside who can provide advice and constructive information.

"It's always good to have this outside impartial party telling you that you're wrong when you're wrong, and telling you you're right when you're right, and giving you the kind of the information and advice that you need, because typically in conflicts like this, particularly in my case, the biggest problem was that we didn't have a tiebreaker vote. It's like he said/she said."

Prior to the conflict, Patel hadn't had a mentor pool or a network of people to turn to for advice. He now belongs to a CEO organization and is actively involved with a network of colleagues.

In the end, Patel purchased his partner's interest. Although he didn't lose the business, he paid much more than the purchase price.

"I don't know what kind of price tag you can put on not being there for your wife and kids," Patel says. "When you're in the situation, you really don't realize what the cost is to those around you. You're still resisting their advice and you might be saying it's temporary, I can work through it, I'm tougher than this.

"At the end of the day, you realize that—in my case, my son is five years old and the other is now three—so from zero to four and from zero to two, you blink an eye and boom, it's like four years gone or two years gone with your kids, and you're just not there," Patel says.

"You're just not there for them because you just don't have any more to give. You've drained yourself emotionally, and you've left it all at work, because you had to be the combatant, and you had to go through the toxicity.

"I can only imagine what kind of father or husband I could have been, if I hadn't been emotionally bankrupt."

Patel says he, his family, and his business have entered a happier and more fruitful phase.

"I've become more direct with people. Basically, if something doesn't seem right, I'm more prone to tell them now up front. I've also taken time to acknowledge those around me more than I have in the past."

The crisis and its attendant soul-searching have changed the way he looks at his life and his business.

"It makes your life lighter; and you really can do more. You might be surprised, because when you're lighter, when you're happier, when you're more emotionally charged, it's surprising," he says. "I mean, now our business is doing much better. We're more focused, we're achieving more than we did in the past, and probably we're doing it with less. We're doing more with less, but it's a direct result of how you actually operate and how you feel about the company.

"When you don't respect and when you don't honor, then at some point you don't even trust, then it's a recipe for disaster. Luckily, things worked out; but in hindsight, just knowing that if I even had shut it down, I would have been in a better place.

"You need to know just when to say 'Enough,' otherwise what happens is you keep hoping, hoping, hoping, and hope is really not the strategy that is going to get you to the other side."

3

HOW DOES FAMILY FIT IN?

Barely...

READ THE SIGNS: DANGER AHEAD

The market will provide obstacles in your business, and there will be variables beyond your control every day at work. You may have predicted some of these. What you probably have not expected is the effect that starting and running your own business will have on your family life. Simply put, it may wreak havoc in a previously quiet predictable place. You are asking a stranger to live with you in your home. By being an entrepreneur, you have invited a new level of risk and possible financial loss into your family's life. You may lose your health too and wind up with nothing more than medical bills and other debts. Unlikely you say? It happens all the time.

Your business will also put new and unusual types of pressure on your existing relationships. You may lose your spouse. You may lose touch with your children and become estranged from your parents and friends. When my wife, Sara, became pregnant in 1995 with our second child, I was literally unconscious. Between the business and the physical stress of running it, I wasn't mentally or physically there. Unlike the pregnancy of our first child, where we shared each growing moment,

Sara had to go through this one alone. Although I was there for the birth, she was saddled with most of the responsibility for the first few months of my son's life. Simply put, this severely strained our relationship. Many times I think it was only her strength and conviction that saved our family bonds. I have always cherished Sara's unwavering support of my energy. I have always admired her way of accepting almost any situation.

During many of these years, my children's activities were a blur to me. I was physically there at many of the important events. But pictures of me show a very hallow and vacant look in my eyes. Sadly, you could see that I was somewhere other than where I was shown to be in the picture.

During this time, relationships with my friends dwindled. I had no time or energy to devote to them. Only my best friend, Zane, remained in my life as a result of Monday evening racquetball games and his constant inquiries about how I was doing. He seemed to be monitoring my actions to make sure I didn't fall too far away.

I protected my parents from most of what was going on. But soon after my stepfather-in-law, Mike Cooper, passed away in October 1998, my mother-in-law became less supportive. Mike, a great entrepreneur who was also one of my mentors, always was able to translate and explain to my mother-in-law what I was doing. After he died, this filtering mechanism was gone. On many occasions she suggested that I abandon the ship and leave my business. She wanted me to find a job so my family would not go hungry or have no place to live. From her perspective, this was the logical thing to do. But I did not see a way out at this time. I had to stay onboard.

Your **B**usiness **I**s the **S**tranger at the **T**able

HAVE A BUSINESS FIRST, THEN HAVE A FAMILY?

In their plan of life, some people will say that they will start a business first when they have no responsibility or family to care for. They have this well-thought-out plan that they will perfectly execute. Although it is true that it is financially easier to do it this way, many entrepreneurs simply have no choice. Typically, you do not get to pick the timing for starting this type of adventure. Instead, the circumstances pick you. I wasn't ready to start a business when I first graduated from college. I wanted a job working for someone else. I wanted the structure provided by a large company. Ten years later, once I had a support structure of friends and family, I was able to go out and launch a business.

In fact, without family support, launching a business can be more lonely and difficult. You have no limiting factors to working endlessly all the time. You have no support structure to come home to at night. There is no one to pick you up when you are down. The hard-fought victories can be less sweet when no one knows the intimate details of what it took to get there.

You Can't Always Plan It

"My fiancé and I are both in agreement. We are both 39, and we both want children. If we want to have children, we also want to make the commitment to each other."

"To be an entrepreneur is very lonely and thrilling as well. When I see a situation and see it growing in my head, there is no one else who can do anything with it except me. I have this vision and I must follow it."

"If you have a partner, then you have to take that part of you and instill it in them. I will do anything to do my films. But I have decided also that I do not want to lose her."

"Then I began to look at it differently. OK, so it's not an either-or thing. If I want to have the relationship, I need to have a different game plan. So it opened things up for me. The worst that can happen is that I fail. There's a fine line between being selfish and having a volcanic drive."

Richard Cohen

YOUR BUSINESS TAKES YOUR FAMILY HOSTAGE

Starting and running a business is a family event. It is not just you out on your own as the lone warrior trying to slay the dragon. You will need the support of your family to get you through the hard times and celebrate the good times with you. Without their strong support you're probably doomed.

Being the spouse of an entrepreneur is especially difficult. He or she is along for the ride, but remember your car is bouncing all over that winding mountainous road. You are driving, which is hard enough, and you are probably not asking for directions. Your spouse, on the other hand, is sitting in the same car with you but in the backseat. To make it worse, your spouse is sitting backward and blindfolded. You thought driving was difficult but just try sitting in the backseat! In my more contemplative moments, I could not understand how my wife was able to do this with me. Although she will readily admit that she is no Florence Nightingale, I still think that she may be Joan of Arc. Sometimes I think she stayed with me against her better judgment. It takes a very special person to build a life with an entrepreneur. You can try to make sure that he or she is the type of person who can go along for the ride, but as with everything else, you will not know until you get there if you have this type of mate. Even a spouse who is very supportive in other situations might crack under this type of stress.

Manish Patel, CEO of Where2GetIt, says that he has caused his wife, Dolly, plenty of mental anguish. "The line between our business life and personal life was not just blurred, it was obliterated," he states. "The entrepreneur's spouse is hidden in the shadows, toiling away and holding things together, never quite getting the credit or recognition she deserves."

Natalie Tessler started Spa Space a few years ago, after she quit working as an attorney at Katten Muchin Zavis Rosenman. She thinks of her business as a baby, too, but one with a lot of colic! Tessler describes the business owner as one who loves her baby "because it is an extension of her, and it becomes the center of her life, but it can also make her crazy. For the husband, it's like being a stepparent. He has to live with the child and share his spouse's time and attention with the child, but he must be careful when giving advice or trying to help, even though he may be tempted to jump right in.

"Because the 'child' is so important to the spouse," Tessler says, "she is likely to be very sensitive to criticism about how she is raising the child. Yet she needs his help and support, so he must develop intuition about when to get involved, when to stay out of it, when to talk about it, and when to drop the subject."

Jeff Richmond is an engineer who became an entrepreneur when he started Pumpbiz. His spouse, Mary Beth, a Chicago physician, says that she always envisioned a successful businessman talking about his wife at their 25th wedding anniversary, proudly boasting, "And how can I ever thank my wife who has been at my side every step of the way and has never, for one minute, doubted me or lost faith in me or failed to support me during all the ups and downs." Then she hits the fast-forward button to her future 25th wedding anniversary and confesses that "Jeff can never say that about me . . . because I have had my doubts, I have lost my faith (not in him but in his endeavor) at times, and I have failed to show unfailing support many times. Trust me, there have been, oh, too many times when I've showed him all my doubts, insecurities, and, yes, even gotten plenty upset at him for taking this road."

If you can, give your spouse lots of latitude to scream and yell. Your spouse might cry, become upset, and question his or her own sanity for continuing with you. He or she has every right to feel this way. This is natural and happens to all of us. Sometimes I wish there were a chapter of Entrepreneurs Anonymous similar to other addiction groups for spouses. I think it could help a lot!

Don't **T**ie the **B**lindfold **T**oo **T**ightly

WHO WANTS TO RELIVE THEIR DAY?

Most entrepreneurs don't tell their spouses on a daily basis how things are going in the business. The ups and downs are just too varied and the swings too wild. How can you explain the drastic difference between the good and bad times and all the subtleties that go into each business event? When my wife would ask, "How was your day, honey?" most days were just too painful to relive or to talk about. There were a lot of days I wanted to forget. Unfortunately, I was forced to relive some of these days in my own dreams at night.

For all the days I did not want to relive, there were also good days that I celebrated with my family. Make a point to do this. It may never balance out with the days when you simply "Don't want to talk about it," but it will remind you of your source of passion and why you got started in the first place. It will also provide an important reconnection point with your family that is important to you.

Celebrate the **S**pecial **D**ays

BORROWING FROM FAMILY
AND FRIENDS—WHOA!

Most of us don't have enough personal money to start a business. Invariably, we ask our family and friends for money to start our businesses. This happens all the time, is a logical stage of the funding process, and is the way businesses have been started throughout history. At the early stages of your business, there is no one else to go to except those you know and those who love you. Additionally, only those who know and love you will give you money to start this crazy adventure. Accept it, but take the money knowing the risks.

Most entrepreneurs lose the money given to them by their friends and family.

You must understand the strings that come attached to the money. It forever changes your relationship with the people who lent it to you. You have crossed a line that is difficult to come back from. Although they gave you the money because they loved and cared about you, they still want it back. This is a fact, regardless of what they say to you.

In the 1980s, I invested $2,000 in a mail-order business that a relative started. I had a little extra money, and it seemed like a good idea at the time. I invested simply because my relative asked me and that was reason enough. A few years later, I received a letter from him sent to all shareholders saying that the business was bankrupt and was going out of business. I was willing to take this risk when I invested the money, but when it actually happened I was not prepared for how it would affect our relationship.

Acknowledge the Risks and Remember the Strings

BORROWING THROWS EMOTIONAL
SUPPORT OUT THE WINDOW

When you take money for your company from your family and friends, your relationship with them will change because you never again will be able to tell them the truth of how your business is going. Imagine your good friend, Ethan, who works as a photographer for a large magazine, just invested in your business. He calls you on a particularly bad day and asks how things are going in your business. What will you say? Will you tell him how you truly feel? Will you say, "Hi Ethan, things are going really bad. I feel like giving up and closing the business."

I don't think so.

When asked how things are going you will say "Fantastic" not wanting Ethan to know that his investment in your business is in danger. Unfortunately, as a result of having this business and his money, you will also have lost a friend who could possibly support you. One entrepreneur says it is like putting the umbilical cord that binds two friends together on a chopping block where it can be severed forever by any poor business result.

I was stung by this once. A friend of mine invested $25,000 in one of my businesses in 1992. I continually told her that she should invest in the business because she believed in it not just because she believed in me. She said that she did believe in the business. A few months later when I was kicked out of this business by my other two partners, and they subsequently went out of business, she blamed me for losing her money. We have not spoken since that day.

A*nd* I*t* C*ould* B*e* G*one* F*orever*

YOUR BUSINESS SLEEPS IN YOUR BED WITH YOU

For the entrepreneur, small business is always personal. It expresses your life energy in the world. The business becomes who you are, who you want to be, and who you are afraid to be. All these come out during the business life cycle.

At the same time, although your passion may be your business, it is important to remember that you are not your business, but your business is part of you every day. The popular belief in our society always pushes to separate our personal and professional lives. We continually hear the refrain that "You shouldn't bring work home with you." Yet, with the days of e-mail, cell phones, and other instantaneous communications upon us, this has become increasingly improbable for most people in all sizes of business. Just look at how common the use of the term *24/7* is, which signifies that we are always accessible.

Never being able to "be away" from your business can profoundly impact your life. The ability of technology always to "find you" through a cell phone call or e-mail can be very detrimental. Is there ever a time where you can just get away? The drive to and from work in a car or on a train used to be that oasis between work and home where you were alone to transition between the two parts of your day. No one knew exactly where you were. Cell phones have obviously eliminated this, and, in fact, I save a lot of my phone callback time specifically for these times when I am unable to answer e-mail or surf the Web. Always being on and connected also strains your ability to get away and rest your mind to focus on other things. It can severely deplete your energy. For a long time, I did not want to have a computer in my house for this very reason. One of the most effective ways to torture prisoners is to limit their ability to sleep by constantly interrupting them. Sound familiar in the business world?

While this electronic umbilical cord has many benefits, it also has been detrimental to businesspeople in our society. It makes it more difficult to do one thing at a time. When was the last time you were in the car and were not talking on the cell phone?

Without cell phones or computers, things moved more slowly. We could focus on one thing at a time because we were not bombarded constantly by interruptions. Incoming phones calls and e-mails did not disrupt our meetings and our dinners. When we were in one place, we were there for better or worse. This is different than today. Standing in line at the post office, I am not just waiting to get some stamps. I am talking on the phone and answering my e-mail. When it becomes my turn, I sometimes forget why I am there.

So what is the solution? Set integrated boundaries for yourself. These can be times during the day or physical places in your life that you go. I do not eliminate cell phones or eliminate e-mailing while on vacation or on various days of the weekend. I tried it and it doesn't work for me. Being away from it makes me think and worry even more about what is going on at work. I'd rather just stay in touch, face the issues, and then forget about them until the next time I check in. On vacation, I check only in the evening. In my daily life, there are cell-free and computer-free zones. I never use a computer or cell phone in my bedroom, at the karate school, at the health club while working out, or at the spa. These are my islands of comfort when my mind rests. No matter what happens while I am in these places, I simply do not care. In this world of instant communication, it is important to have times during your daily routine when whatever is happening at a particular moment can wait.

A*nd* I*t* H*ogs the* C*overs*

YOUR BUSINESS CAN— AND WILL—MAKE YOU SICK!

In May 1995, I awoke one morning and my vision was blurry. I thought I was sick or my glasses were dirty. The next day I awoke and it was worse. I consulted my doctor. I thought I was going blind. I called my ophthalmologist and waited for an appointment. I remember sitting in my living room clinging to my young son because I could not see him well. After the doctor examined my eyes and could find nothing wrong, he said I probably had diabetes. I was amazed. I was 35, not overweight, without a history of the disease in my family. How could I have diabetes? Unfortunately, hospital tests later confirmed his diagnosis. The doctors told me that diabetes at this age can come from the stress. Did all the ups and downs of running my business kill the beta cells in my pancreas so they could not make insulin?

I sat in the waiting room reading a thick medical textbook about diabetes the doctor had given me. I read all the complications that would ultimately afflict me: blindness, heart attacks, amputation, and kidney disease. I would have to measure and weigh carefully all the food I ate and record it in a little book. I would have to check my blood sugar every four hours. Doing this would keep my blood sugars under control and delay the inevitable complications. No problem, I thought. I was a survivor. I would see my kids grow up; or maybe I would not. I had never had to face anything like this. As I waited for my wife, I cried.

Because blood sugar rises only when a person eats something, I reasoned that if I did not eat, my blood sugar would not go up. I measured every spoonful of food. As a result, my blood sugar did stay under control, but I also lost 30 percent of my body weight (52 pounds) in two months. Most of my friends thought I was dying of AIDS. I looked and felt sicker than before I found out I had diabetes. This plunged me into a downward spiral of depression, anorexia, and anxiety. For almost a year, I could not enjoy eating. I was in a dark room that had no door. I thought that the business passion that had once inspired me, eventually would kill me.

During these times, my family and friends supported me. The faces of my children sustained me. Some great pharmaceutical drugs eased me up out of this tremendous hole. If it were not for all these things working together, I surely would not have survived.

During this time, my business partner did a great job of carrying the load. In a strange way, I was still able to go to work and be productive. At least at work I could face real things that caused anxiety and try to solve them from the logical side of the brain. While my business may have been the poison that got me sick, it also was something to sustain me while I struggled to get better.

It Also Carries You While You Heal

"I never believed in worrying. And having a business definitely affected that. During the process of building the spa, I could not sleep. Before that, I was never a high anxiety person."

"The other thing that can make you sick is having investors. On one hand, you feel so incredibly grateful to these people. They are the people who are facilitating and enabling you to live out your dream. For me, they are like angels in my life. I feel so grateful that these people believe in me and trust me enough to invest their faith and their money in me."

"On the other hand, knowing that they are out there is bedeviling because I feel so indebted and so concerned about any failure that I may have and how they'll respond to it."

"In some ways it's not about the money. It is about this emotional gift they gave me in believing in me. It's really scary to think that I could let them down. And that makes my stomach twist and turn."

Natalie Tessler

HAPPILY SUCCESSFUL MEANS MERGING PERSONAL AND PROFESSIONAL

You not only need to bring your work home with you, you need to fully integrate your business and professional lives to reach your goal. You can't necessarily control your goal of financial success. What you can control is how the combination of your personal and professional lives brings energy into your life. It is important to focus on being "happily successful" regardless of the financial success in your business. How can I enjoy my business most days, regardless of whether I make a million dollars? How can my personal life benefit from integrating my business with my life?

If you have the passion to run a business, you can't but help to bring business into your personal life. Combine these two lives or perish!

I used to try to compartmentalize my business and personal lives. No work after 6 PM, no work on weekends, no e-mail on vacation. I spent so much of that time wondering what was going on at work that I was still unable to enjoy my time away from work. When I combined work and play, I could have one life no matter where I was or what I was doing.

I am not suggesting that you should always carry your laptop or cell phone with you. It amazes me when I see people talking on cell phones while standing at bathroom urinals or pedaling on exercise bikes. I think this can lead to additional problems. You need to carve out "no-work time zones" for yourself and family.

Carve **O**ut **N**o-**W**ork **T**ime **Z**ones

NOT THE FAMILY ENTREPRENEURIAL TEST

Do your family and friends have what it takes to survive your starting and growing a business? Again, there is no test that they can take. You won't know until you are there. Even having your spouse talk to other spouses of entrepreneurs does not help. They will never believe any of these things can happen to them.

But going through this with your friends and family is not a bad thing. It is an opportunity to strengthen the bonds among you. It is a way to face real-life tests together. With my wife and family, I am sure we probably don't cherish everything we went through. But it has helped us discover more parts of who we are and has drawn us closer in many ways. We have survived together, and that prepares us for other things that may come with a bit more confidence.

Y*ou* S*core* E*xtra for* S*urvival*

"You choose to learn from pain."

Suzi Bonk

THE LOVABLE, TOOTHLESS, AND IMPOVERISHED ENTREPRENEUR

So then what does your family have to gain? You may say long-term wealth and security, but as I have described, the odds are against you. If this doesn't happen, what else is in it for your family? First, admit to yourself that you are starting or running this business for you, not for your family. There are probably easier ways to monetarily support your family. You are following the path you designed, and it doesn't necessarily include others. Always remember that this is your fantasy, not theirs.

If riches never come, your family can still grow from this journey. In the long run they gain a better, more complete you who has tested your mettle and stood at the edge and jumped. They see a person with fewer regrets and a fuller life. They see someone who can pass lessons on to his or her children with more wisdom and courage. A person who has supported his or her family despite the odds can really be called a lovable winner.

One daily event can warm your heart during barren emotional times. Singing my kids to sleep at night was that time for me. Despite my absence physically and emotionally during the entire day, I had that one quiet moment when I put them to bed most nights. I would cradle them in my arms, put pacifiers in their mouths. I would softly sing lyrics of songs I had made up. I would look deeply into their eyes and exchange all types of thoughts without ever talking. Sometimes I would comfort them in the middle of the night, even though they yelled for mom. These small moments formed an unbreakable bond in our relationships.

Apply a Heart-Warmer at Least Once a Day

A True Tale
STEPHANIE COVALL-PINNIX
Choosing between Your Two Families

Stephanie Covall-Pinnix and her team at Triton-Tek really had the mojo. When they were on a roll, they didn't have to talk. They could almost read one another's minds.

"It's like when you're married to somebody, where you can finish the other person's sentence," Covall-Pinnix says. "So the mojo would be that we were sitting in a meeting with a company that had a problem, and immediately we could identify what the problem was, and without talking, either George or Carl or myself would know innately who was going to answer the question based on what the problem was.

"That person would start talking," Covall-Pinnix says. "And then other people would interject, and it would just be like this amazing conversation. Right at the end you propose a solution, and I would say we had a 95 percent close rate. It was crazy."

The team had no need to huddle. No need to consult offstage. They would simply pull together seamlessly to create a solution.

"I was able to bring opportunity to the table, and I could interpret what the other person wanted and explain it to George and Carl," Covall-Pinnix says.

"George was more like a regular, very down-to-earth person and not as technical as Carl. But Carl was like a physicist. . . . He would never talk until right at the end of the meeting. Then he would start drawing on the whiteboard whatever the solution was going to be. Then I would close the meeting."

Covall-Pinnix had come a long way from her roots in Yakima, Washington, to work the mojo in the boardrooms of Chicago. She had hit the road early when her parents divorced. With only a high school diploma, she took whatever work she could find. She had worked at a Sizzler's restaurant, conducted surveys in malls for a market research company, and for a short time, when her life fell apart, lived in a car. She was 21 when she became pregnant and went to live in the projects of Yakima. But when her baby daughter was born, Covall-Pinnix finally had an anchor of passion in her life that could propel her forward.

"I wanted to be the best single parent I could," Covall-Pinnix says. "I got a job working for Washington State. I was hired by a man whose mom was a single mom."

Working for the state, Covall-Pinnix pulled her life together. It was during this time that she met her husband, Jack, a college professor. "I just wanted to date a nice person," she says. He asked her to marry him and she did. Soon they all moved to Chicago when he started attending the University of Chicago.

Transplanted to Chicago's Hyde Park, Covall-Pinnix landed a job at J. P. Morgan Securities in the fixed-income department. She was 23 when she found herself on her first-ever business trip, walking overwhelmed and homesick, through the caverns of Wall Street in New York City.

It was in 1993 at J. P. Morgan that Covall-Pinnix discovered she had a knack for technology. She found that she was good at training people. And because she hated wasting paper, soon all her department's fixed-income customers had CompuServe accounts and access to an online library of information. Before too long, Covall-Pinnix was no longer the secretary and was instead hiring her own assistant. Her active networking was bringing in leads for business, and it was during this time her career in technology sales took off, leading to senior positions with an Oracle database development and data warehouse consultancy, and with RCN/21st Century/EnterAct.

It was after these solid years of selling and business development that Covall-Pinnix took the bait to become an entrepreneur.

During all her time in technology and throughout her life, Covall-Pinnix had mixed business friends with personal friends. She found herself introducing people to one another. Because she spent so much time working, she liked to bring all her friends together.

RCN was going through a lot of change, and two former members of Covall-Pinnix's consulting team at RCN—who had now become two of her closest friends—had started a company, Triton-Tek. They offered her a spot with it.

"I had been going back and forth and talking about [leaving RCN and going to Triton-Tek] for weeks and agonizing. Finally, one day at RCN, they offered me yet another position. . . . I'm like, 'You know what? I'm going to get paid an ungodly amount of money to do nothing,' and I just felt like I couldn't do that.

"So I really didn't have a chance to talk to my husband. My husband always says, 'Whatever your decision is, I'll support you.' So I decided that afternoon. I just quit," Covall-Pinnix says.

"I was so happy just to leave. I had been upset for weeks, and then as soon as I made my decision, I was so happy," Covall-Pinnix says. "It was a decision that I just made instantly, and I instantly felt the weight of the world shifting."

Covall-Pinnix had helped the partners put the business together, but she wasn't on the payroll yet. When she called to tell them she was onboard, they were surprised and delighted because just a few weeks earlier she had declined to join them.

"I had told them initially I wasn't going to do it," she says, "because I was really afraid that things wouldn't turn out, and we wouldn't be friends. We had such good energy as businesspeople together, and I was concerned because the market was shifting and the economy was shifting, and I wasn't sure if it was the best time to be starting a company.

"But I trusted them, and they trusted me," she says. "[I told them] I will do whatever it takes to be sure that the company will stay afloat, and I'd do whatever is necessary to make that possible, but I have very much a survivalist mentality. When I sense that there is going to be a huge conflict, I will leave the situation."

The year was 2001, and Covall-Pinnix was concerned that the pressure-cooker economy was going to add an additional layer of stress, which could lead to tension and fighting. But this time, there would be no other department to blame or to transfer anger and frustration to—there would just be each other. Also, she was at times uncomfortable with the mentality of some engineers, who could be harsh and judgmental with nonengineers without even realizing it.

"It's the same thing in life," Covall-Pinnix says. "If you look at kids in school, there's going to be a class clown. There's going to be the person who's the most popular that everybody wants to emulate. There's going to be the nerd.

"In business, there's going to be a leader, there's going to be the geek, there's going to be the person that is probably smart, but everybody gets mad at because he or she is indecisive." Covall-Pinnix says. "It's just the group mentality.

"I'm the person that always is very decisive and gets things done, and that's how we get along," Covall-Pinnix says. "I tell them what to do."

About eight months into the business, the partners needed to figure out where the business was going, but nobody was being decisive.

"Nobody could come to agreement on anything because we were partners and nobody wanted to fight," Covall-Pinnix says. "And I am saying, 'Somebody needs to be making decisions.'"

With some outside advice, the Triton-Tek team decided Covall-Pinnix would be CEO.

"Everybody was a little tense about it, but at the same time, it was a bit of a relief because somebody was finally going to be responsible," Covall-Pinnix says. "Running the company was the hardest thing and the funniest thing that I had ever done."

Eventually, however, the communication breakdown Covall-Pinnix had feared would occur did occur.

"I'll talk and say, 'I sense that you're upset about something,' and try to get it resolved," Covall-Pinnix says. "In that office we had 1,000 square feet. There were six of us, and we all sat within 5 feet of one another. When somebody was upset with somebody about some small thing, everybody knew.

"When I became the CEO, I moved across the office, away from everybody else, because I just could not deal with that negative energy," Covall-Pinnix says. "If you're trying to push your idea forward and make sales and have a good face on things, you can't be sitting in this negative pot of stew.

"It was like a big dysfunctional family," Covall-Pinnix says. "Somebody needs to be in charge right from the beginning. So making that shift in the middle was really hard.

"That's when the mojo went away," she says. "It was like a death."

There's a saying—expect the unexpected. Sometimes the unexpected is good, sometimes it's bad. In Covall-Pinnix's case, it was bad, very bad. Her husband became ill.

"My husband was sick," she says. "It was pretty much negative and stressful on all aspects of my life, and I was just starting to melt down. I just couldn't do that to my partners, and I couldn't do that to my husband, because he needed me to be strong. So it was just easier for me to leave.

"Everybody was sad," Covall-Pinnix says. "We all cried, but that's just the way it works out."

Covall-Pinnix left Triton-Tek in the summer of 2002 reluctantly and with great sadness. "My husband is better now. My family won out over everything.

"People always said to me business isn't personal, but business is personal," Covall-Pinnix says. "It was so painful because these were the people I had developed the product with over four years. I always felt that we were invincible. That we could do anything."

In the end, Covall-Pinnix says it was the pull of her family that forced the decision.

"My daughter, last year I think she called me eight times from school to go and pick her up because she was sick," Covall-Pinnix says.

"Really, I found out at the end, she was like, 'Mom, you're just never home, and the only way that I know that I'll see you is if I pretend to be sick.'

"She's going to be 13 next month," Covall-Pinnix says, "and you know, when your child who's getting to be a teenager says that she wants you home for dinner, you're like, 'OK.'"

Soon after leaving Triton-Tek, Covall-Pinnix joined SGS Net as the Director of Business Development. Still, she continues to be on the board of directors of Triton-Tek and keeps her eyes open for opportunities.

4

FIND THE LUNATICS
LIKE YOU!

Team Building for the Rest of Us

IT'S WHO, NOT WHAT

Iwish I had learned a long time ago that it is who you are working with, not what you are doing with them. Things would have been easier for me, and I would have saved myself a lot of sleepless nights. I never dreamt about a single business idea. I always dreamt about the people involved with my company. The idea for your business really means nothing. The type of business you are in will not contribute at all to being "happily successful." What will mean everything is the people you are working with and how they are able to execute any given business idea.

It happens all the time. People ask if I think they have a good business idea. I don't even wait to even hear the idea anymore. My answer is always the same, "I have absolutely no idea."

I say this because just to have an idea for a business is meaningless. Anyone can have a great idea or a terrible one that, on its own, seems like a great or a bad business. As an angel investor, many people want me to sign a confidentiality agreement before they will share their business plan with me. They are afraid that someone will take their idea and use it. Investors never do. In fact, I always tell them that ten people in this country are probably thinking of their exact idea at this very moment. I agree with Bill Reichert, Managing Director of Garage Venture Technologies, who says to entrepreneurs "Someone else has already stolen this idea and your next one too."

People, Not Ideas, Are Unique

"I don't care if you know no one, if you can meet the right people, and I don't mean well connected—I just mean smart and friendly and resourceful and creative—they will end up being interested in what you're trying to do. There isn't any technology or any financial backing that will compensate for bad people, and good people can compensate for all of those things."

Liz Ryan

THE PEOPLE MEAN EVERYTHING

It was 1991, and I had just been fired. I was done working for someone else. I wanted to devote my energies to starting my own business. But I had one problem: I did not have a business idea or anyone to go into business with. So, I looked in the classified section of a local business publication. I thought that finding a business was like shopping for a used car! What I found were two people seeking financial capital and a third partner. I qualified for both.

Over the next few weeks I met with these partners and learned about their start-up business. They seemed like nice guys. The technology was innovative, and, in fact, it amazed me. I checked their references. I was sure it would be a hit. I invested all my family's savings, which included all the money from our wedding gifts, and money my wife had received when her father had died in a car accident. I even got some of our friends to help fund the company.

Within a month, I knew I had made a mistake. My partners and I could not agree on anything. The two original partners were friends, and I was always the odd man out. I was still excited about the technology but working with my two partners made it awful. A year after I began, and one month before my first child was born, they surprised me by kicking me out of my company without notice. They said good-bye and kept my money. I had suspected for a long time that I had made a mistake. I had been thinking that I had gone into business with the wrong people. This confirmed it.

The Wrong People Can Cost You Everything

FOLLOW THE STREAM OF PEOPLE

Here I was now, recently married, months from being a father, unemployed, and broke. Life could only be described as a mess. While my best friend, Zane, who is an attorney, battled to get my money back, I became sick over the stress and stayed in bed. Later, my first son was born. Weeks after that, I started another business with the money Zane was able to retrieve for me. Soon after, a business associate and friend of mine had an idea and a plan. I had time, business desire, and a child to support. Although I was not exactly "tanned and rested," I was ready to go.

But this time, I started a company with a guy I had known for years, a person I had conducted business with in the past. Although I felt the business area was boring, I knew this guy. I knew his wife. I respected their family. He was known as a smart and savvy businessperson. We became great partners and grew a strong business together. We hired good people. Strangely enough, as the business grew, I became fascinated and passionate about the industry. This became one of the best professional experiences for me.

When people tell me that they are not sure what kind of business they want to be in professionally, I tell them that they should find a group of people they respect and can learn from. Go work with these people regardless of the type of business they are pursuing. I always say that I could sell chairs if I were doing it with people I respected. I tell them that they should follow the stream of people not the stream of ideas. Remember that who you are in business with is more important than what business you are in.

*When You Find the Right People,
Stick with Them*

COMFORT IN SIMILAR
SUCCESSES AND FAILURES

People love to win together. Just watch a sports team after winning a championship game. Then go into the losers' locker room. Much more subtle is the behavior of people who have lost together. Although you won't see these people slapping each other on the back and pouring champagne over one another's heads, they are still bound together by their failure. They have shared a common experience and can appreciate each other. If these people only lose together, then this is a bad thing. When they get together, they will feel like only one thing: like a loser. But if they can win and lose, they can get more tightly bound together. But if people only win together, winning does not bind them forever. After a while, they will take winning for granted and think that each of them separately is responsible for the team's success. This is why it is so difficult for sports teams to put consecutive championship years together back-to-back. But if the team of people can win and lose together, then they can experience both in a more rounded experience.

The entrepreneur can do best by finding a group of people who can happily succeed and fail together. You high-five and feel proud about your success. You share blame and commiserate after your failures, vowing to redouble your effort and try to win again. You and your team are humbled. Have you noticed that the victories always feel sweeter after you have failed? If you can find comfort with a team who succeeds and fails together, you can truly call yourself winners no matter what happens.

With the **R**ight **P**eople **Y**ou **A**lways **W**in

BIRDS OF A FEATHER HANG TOGETHER

To accomplish great things in business, it usually takes a team of people to get it done. Few Lone Rangers can be successful at business. While every business needs a leader, every great entrepreneur needs a team to execute the plan. You will not survive going it alone. When things get tough, the other team members can keep it going. This is why

S u z i   B o n k

A venture capital firm offered Suzi Bonk some cash, but only if she would move her business, SofaLogic, to Toronto or Montreal from Winnipeg. She said no.

She didn't want to leave the people who had been working with her as volunteers for years. And she did not want to rebuild a community of colleagues in a new city. The repercussion of her decision was that she was calling it quits for her business.

Bonk's decision underscores the value people play in a start-up: how much they mean to the entrepreneur, and how much they will give when they share your passion.

"Entrepreneurs have to hold ourselves to a higher standard," she says. "They [other team members] are not just coming onboard because they are crazy, they are coming onboard because they believe in you, and they believe in this idea that you call a business.

"Part of being an entrepreneur is selling an idea," she says. "In that kind of boom [1999] period, people convinced other people to work with them for equity in the company. Equity doesn't mean anything until the company has real value, and that can be 10 years down the road.

"When you recruit someone, you have to be very realistic about whether something is going to work or not. You owe them," she says. "You need to keep them appraised of what is really happening. Those people will sign up again," she says. "Those lunatics will do it again, if you are honest with them.

"Look at them as people who are crazy enough to come along," she says. "On their path, they are working for free. They are sacrificing their time and energy. They are looking for you to treat them fairly. What you tell them, how transparent you are really speaks more about you than anything else that you do.

"They are there because they have trust in you," she says. "There is a joint dream."

in so many successful start-ups some people have always worked together before. Successful teams of folks stay together because they have no learning curve and they have a deep-seated sense of trust. They know one another's strengths and weaknesses, so they are able to complement each other. Because they know one another's roles, they can almost predict the other person's moves. They can fill in gaps where one is weak and lead the charge where another is strong. There is a comfort in having been in business with the same people before. There is no substitute for working with someone you have worked with previously. You have been successful together before, and you have confidence as a team to do it again.

Rick Mazursky is the former CEO of VTech. He has more than 30 years' experience in creating and marketing consumer products and taking them from ideas to manufacturing to sales. As the CEO of VTech in the 1990s, he grew the business from a struggling midsize company to one of the top toy companies in the world. Whenever he starts working at a new place, he brings trusted members of other teams to be with him. He has used the same vice president of sales at three different companies. For the past 15 years, he has used the same product development manager, graphic artists, packaging specialists, and model makers across many projects. In turn, all these people have used the same teams: the same sales force, ad agency, product developers, factories. It works.

T *here* I *s* a "**U**" *in* T *eam*

FACING THE ENEMY TESTS THE TEAM

How can you tell if the team is right? Does it just feel right or is it magic? Is it the books, movies, and music that you all like together? The reader may want each member of their prospective team to take a ten-question test to see if they are compatible with each other. Again, there isn't one just like there isn't one for marriage. You can only determine if you have a good team or a good partner after you have gone through the business experience together.

Only weathering good and bad times will test your team, and either bind people together or propel them apart. Men and women in military combat easily share this feeling. They have faced a common enemy. You will know when it doesn't work. You will argue with your other team members on who will do what and how to proceed. You will trip over each other with different intentions. If this happens, admit it to yourself and find other people. You will also know when it works. It's like actors in a play, musicians in an orchestra, and dancers at the ballet. A new energy is created from your team that did not exist before. You will smile to yourself knowing you can accomplish great things and face additional difficulties. Indeed you can.

With the **R**ight **T**eam **Y**ou **C**an **F**ace **A**nything

CAN'T WE ALL JUST GET ALONG?

Personal belief and passion in your business idea is only one part of the equation. Can you get along with and believe in the people you are signing on to work with? The optimist in me always wondered why people in this world could not all get along. When I started to run companies 15 years ago, I began to understand why we all couldn't get along. In any group, people look for reasons to band together for support. This usually takes the form of separating out others or singling people out. These actions unfortunately enable the people in the accusing group to raise themselves up and feel better by making others feel worse.

I always marveled at the fact that when I had 30 people in a single office, they would find the silliest ways to separate themselves. It wasn't always the traditional company divisions—things like the salespeople disliking the marketing people or the finance group at odds with the operations team. It took a different twist. The people in the back of the office didn't like the people in the front of the office because they liked the heat on too high or played their music too loud or kept their desks messy. The strangest arguments arose that I could never predict or prevent.

Whenever there is a group of people, it takes leadership to get them to work well together. Someone has to lead and others have to follow. Without a leader, there is only chaos. A leader is not the person shouting orders to the team members or the person who works 100 hours per week. The leader isn't always the one out front leading the charge and taking all the credit. Your leadership can take many forms.

You Are the Leader—That's Your Job

"It's not just a solo game. You have to check your ego at the door, because once you let your pride get involved, you can kiss your company good-bye. You have to be able to let go, because once you let go and put your faith in others, that's when you can see your company really soar."

"I am just the chief cheerleader, money raiser, the person with the vision. But the people who are working with me are doing the execution, building the business, and holding it together."

Marsha McVicker

LEAD FROM YOUR AUTHENTIC CORE

Leadership is especially difficult in times of ambiguity and rapid change like those that abound in any type of business. During times of conflict and stress it is difficult to lead. Buddhism talks about the concept of Authentic Leadership where the leader's skills drive innovation, while at the same time managing conflict. In Shambhala terms, leadership is based on Authentic Presence, which is where you discover your own intrinsic power and confidence.

In your business, leadership is about risk taking but a different kind than we usually think of. It is easy for the traditional entrepreneur to lead by doing everything himself or herself or by ordering other people to do tasks and then cleaning up after them. You are, however, truly a leader in your business when you can successfully let go and trust other members of your team to do the roles that you have defined together. Without this, all you will ever be is a one-man band, and your business will never grow. Leadership is also about successfully negotiating with your team members the different roles they will take and monitoring how they interact and work with each other. This is difficult, but once you've achieved it, you'll quickly realize why people keep their same teams together through many different business opportunities.

How do you do this? Hire people you have successfully worked with before. If you are hiring new people you do not know, get references on them from people you do know. Make sure your objectives for the overall company goal are clear. Write them down and review them with everyone in the company. Make them simple and to the point so anyone can memorize them! Define each person's role individually and in relation to others in the company. Constantly be involved in the success and failure of these relationships so you can spot any early problems or issues.

It Just Flows

"You can influence, but you can't really control. You can lead, but there's really not much that you can manage. Leadership is acknowledged; management is enforced. And if you have to manage, it will never be as successful as if you're recognized as a leader. That kind of emotional leadership or persuasiveness is much more influential in rallying a team and accomplishing a goal than a manager saying, 'You'll be here at 8:00 tomorrow morning or else.'"

Dave Ormesher

WHEN DYNAMITE FIZZLES

Poor team dynamics are not always easy to spot, especially in a start-up where there is already a lot of chaos. Screaming and yelling are not always telltale signs. It can be difficult to tell the good players from the bad ones. Look at how people get along. Do they try to fill in and compensate for each other? Which people look to place blame instead of accepting failure and looking for solutions. Who is willing to be flexible in his or her role in the company and do whatever must be done to get the job done?

If you find team members or relationships that do not work, do not hesitate to immediately change the people or their roles. People do not typically change much. I always regretted not making changes sooner rather than waiting. You will too.

Make Changes Immediately

HOW DO YOU FIRE YOUR BUSINESS "FAMILY"?

It is difficult to make changes in your business, especially related to people. The idea that a business is a family is cliché. But the fact is that you do get to know people very personally and intricately in a start-up business. You see the same people every day. You meet their families. You are part of their daily routine. When you need to make a change in your company and even fire someone, you will spend a lot of time telling yourself it is his fault. But, ultimately, you were the one who hired him, and it's your responsibility for making the decision that had this outcome. Unlike in a large business, people in a small one are not just numbers on the page. You must sit down with this person and tell him face-to-face. I think that every time I fired someone or had to lay someone off from one of my companies, I got sick. It was always difficult for me because I knew that the person was not going to find a new job right away. Knowing that he had a family to support made it even more difficult. I would go home, and this would haunt me. I used to daydream of his children's faces. Knowing that he wasn't performing or realizing that we had to let him go so the rest of the organization could survive did not make the process any easier. It still sucked every single time.

Do it quickly as soon as you recognize there is a nonfit with your organization. Many times you can tell this in the first 30 days. Don't drag it on. You are not doing the employee any favors. Forget about your pain. Treat them fairly. Pay them what you owe them. Give them as much severance pay as you can afford. Give them a reference letter if appropriate or help them find another job. Apologizing that it did not work out will ease their pain. Doing it this way will ease your pain that you did the right thing.

With Personal Sadness and Pain

"I was making decisions with no grounding in experience. There were many areas that I was weak in, and I did not hire superpeople around me to complement those weaknesses. When you are an entrepreneur everything is personal. When I laid off 100 people, a piece of my soul went with that."

David Weinstein

WHEN TEAM MEMBERS QUIT

Alternatively, I have had times when my best people quit one of my companies without notice. My first reaction was always anger and betrayal. I would wonder how could they do this to me after all we have been through and everything we have achieved? It took me a long time not to look at these situations as personal insults.

I especially hated receiving this type of news by e-mail or voice mail. I thought again it was a personal insult to our relationship. But again, over time, I realized that the individual leaving in this manner was just scared of my reaction and did not know how to break the news to me. Although I still do not think this is the appropriate way to deliver the message, I eventually was able to forgive this method of news delivery as well.

Even though business is personal, a team member leaving is not a betrayal. This person probably appreciates everything your company has done for her. At the same time, the individual must do what is in her own personal and best interest. Unfortunately, sometimes this means leaving your company for what she thinks is a better job. I had to work hard to understand this reality. Similarly, I might face a situation someday where I have to decide whether to fire her so the company and I can survive.

Unless she is going to your chief competitor, wish her well and offer to help. If you worked effectively together, you will have an opportunity to do business together again in the future. Count on it!

Sometimes you can get so ground down by your business on a daily basis that you start to think that everyone is against you. Although the market certainly does not care whether you succeed or fail, it is egotistical to think that it and everyone associated with business is out to get you. It may seem like this on those dark days that I have described, but during more contemplative times you will realize you have allies on your team and customers who want you to succeed.

B *etrayal?* **N** *ot* **R** *eally*

A T r u e T a l e
RICK MAZURSKY *It's All in a Day's Play*

Rick Mazursky was in the toy business for 30 years before he launched his latest creation, PDQ Mazoo, which stands for Pretty Darn Quick Mazoo. Mazoo by the way is the college nickname for Mazursky's son.

PDQ Mazoo is a product-realization company—it takes a product from conception through design to production to make it real. For a good chunk of Mazursky's vastly successful career, he spent 100 days a year working in the Far East developing and selling products. One of his best-known gigs was as President of VTech, which he grew from a $50 million business in the United States to a $180 million business internationally. He was inducted into the Entrepreneurs Hall of Fame for this achievement. Under Mazursky's direction, VTech was at one time the fifth-largest toy company in the world. It also moved into the educational electronics business, starting a children's software company and a computer hardware company.

One aspect of running a business that Mazursky has deep and abiding respect for is building a team.

"You might have a Michael Jordan, but unless you have more strong players around him, you can't win," Mazursky says. "I think the workplace is the same thing. You have to trust one another, or it's not going to work.

"When I came to Vtech it was a company in real trouble," he says. "It was a real struggle. The retail buyers had lost confidence in it. I knew I had to come in and make changes very quickly. The team was young and inexperienced.

"What I had to do was bring in people from my former lives—real pros to augment the existing staff and make it a very congenial group. My former vice president of sales, I brought him in to help organize my sales effort. He, in turn, brought in staff he had used in the past. I brought in a former head of product development who I had hired out of college to put a product development team together."

He also brought outside sources he had used before—an ad agency and a public relations agency.

"When we got it all together," Mazursky says, "everybody felt confident about their other team members—that we would be successful.

The advantage of having loyalty in an ongoing team is that there is virtually no learning curve. Also there is a great sense of trust and everybody feels that we are in a winning situation because we have been in a winning situation together before.

"My senior team members helped to train the younger inexperienced staff," Mazursky says. "We really developed a great company.

"As I move on to other businesses, I still use a lot of the very same people," he says. "Everyone feels very comfortable with one another. Everyone knows where they belong on the team. And everyone understands exactly where they belong in the scheme of things."

5

HAVING A PARTNER

Get Ready for Marriage without Sex

IT'S LONELY AT THE TOP

In 1988, I dreamed of owning my own computer software business, mostly I think, because I wanted to sit in my boss's high-back leather chair. After starting three businesses with a great degree of success and failure, I have found that the saying "It's lonely at the top" is true. I have been there, and it can get darn cold. That's why it can be more rewarding if you have the right partner to travel with you and share the processes of idea generation and decision making.

The question of whether you should form a business with a partner or have a partner join you in an existing business is tricky. As with most business questions, the answer is an unequivocal, "It depends."

A partner gives you someone to share responsibility with so you don't have to bear the entire day-to-day weight of running the company yourself. This can be comforting and supportive. Sometimes two people together are greater than the sum of the whole if they have a synergy of skills. Just as often, two people working together are less than the sum of the whole. Another problem is that, unfortunately, you may not always agree with your partner, and disagreements if not settled can kill your company. If partners don't work equally as hard toward the same goal, conflicts will erupt. Remember that it is far easier to go into business with someone than to get out. The honeymoon phase of any relationship is always more exciting and fun then the daily grind of working together over a period of years.

Getting into a Partnership Is Easier Than Getting Out

FORGET THE FOG. BE HONEST

The first thing you need to look for in a partner are skills that complement your own. If you are good at sales and marketing, team up with someone who is good at technology and operations. This will also provide an easy way to split up the responsibilities in the company once you are both working there. Although you might not always get to choose the person, complementary skills are optimal. Because business is still about people, if you have to make a critical decision on a partner, go with the person you respect and trust over the person with the best skills match. This may sound counterintuitive, but if you have a solid base of business skills with your partner, you can always hire specific skills in your company at another level.

Partners also need to have excellent communication skills and must be able to talk honestly about any issue. This is the only successful method of negotiation. My last partner and I always had a rule that when we had a dispute, we would never be angry with each other for more than 24 hours. You have a critical responsibility never to divulge your personal differences with your partner to the other employees. Never use employees against your partner. This carving up of a company into "loyal gangs" may boost your personal ego but will be detrimental to your business in the long run.

Partners need to be able to argue effectively and stay as close to the facts as you know them. Watch out for a partner who mentions all kinds of nonrelevant information just to win the argument. I have tried both methods of winning an argument and only dealing with relevant business will solve whatever issue you are facing. If every disagreement ends up being a personal attack, you need to look beyond the immediate issues and question the future of your partnership.

It took Jonathan Ginsburg and his partner, Elyse Seabart (not their real names), time to learn this lesson in their business. "The key is you have to have open communication," Ginsburg says. "You have to be able to find some way of having those tough conversations without making it personal. That was one of the toughest things that we came across, where things became very personal."

Conversations would disintegrate into disputes, and a small issue would spiral out of control. "So what you find is that you start having differences of how to do things in the business," Ginsburg says, "and then very quickly it ends up becoming this personal battle about what people are contributing to the business, who's doing the work," he says.

You should also be aware of how your partner reacts when the chips are down. It's easy to be positive and agreeable when things are going well. The test of any partnership is how each person responds when things are going poorly. Each partner needs to support the other during times of crises and not look to place blame on the other person. Both partners should identify what happened and how to fix it, and not dwell on whose fault it is.

Partners must discuss how much money they need to live today and how much they are able to invest in the business. If one partner has other wealth and wants to invest all the profits back into the business instead of taking a salary, this should be addressed right away. Each partner might face different financial pressures that if not discussed ahead of time can cause additional areas of conflict in the future. If one of the partners is unable to pay family bills, he or she will not be effective at work.

You should take certain financial steps prior to forming a business partnership. Decide who will keep track of the money. Just like married couples, most disagreements in a business partnership happen over money. Pick an accountant who has no ties with either partner. Put a good bookkeeping system in place and follow through with its reporting. Most important, review financial statements monthly together and understand where your cash is coming from and going to.

Talk about It Up Front. All of It

ALL PARTNERS ARE NOT CREATED EQUAL

Unlike the guarantee in the American Constitution, all partners are not created equal. No matter how hard you try to divide up the responsibility pie, there will always be times when the work or the effort will seem unequal. This is especially true on a daily basis. Although it may be hard to swallow, take the long view of your business partnership and accept this. Many times one partner will carry the business on his back for a while, and then the other partner may be forced into action. One partner might win a key victory for the company one day and, the next, the other might. Or maybe not.

In 1995 when things were spiraling down for me as a result of diabetes and depression, my partner worked hard and carried our business for more than six months. I am grateful that he accepted that responsibility without even being asked. I believe he did this because he knew that we enjoyed success in the past together, and that if he could hold the business together alone for a bit longer, we could do it again. I am thankful that I had found a partner like this.

Seek some type of balance over a period of years where each partner feels he or she adds a valuable component to the business that the other is unable to bring. If you find yourself feeling that you are always carrying the business, and that your partner does not carry his or her weight, it is important to discuss this with him or her immediately. If these discussions do not resolve the situation, it is time to "file for divorce" from your partnership.

B*ut* **Y***ou* **S***hould* **F***eel the* **B***alance*

PARTNERSHIP IS MARRIAGE WITHOUT SEX

Take my advice. Talk to your attorney and take the necessary legal steps when you have a partner in your business. Partnerships are basically marriages without sex. It is critical to figure out how you will get divorced at the same time you get married in partnership with this person. The stakes are so much lower at the start before you form the business.

S *u z i* **B** *o n k*

Suzi Bonk has been developing an international venture capital fund. She and her business partner had raised $6.5 million, when he became ill and died.

"I learned that nothing is for sure," she says. "Anything can go wrong. You have to recognize that it could be something so unexpected, so unseen that could go wrong. That is the biggest part of the learning process."

"You think that you won't raise enough money. That people won't buy your product," she says. "It never occurs to you that the person who you are working with—that something could happen to them."

"Visionaries cannot be replaced," she says. "In this case, it is virtually impossible to make this business work without him."

"It puts business in perspective," she says. "The privilege of this wasn't the business itself. The privilege was working with him and the learning from him. The value of it was that I got to work with him."

"I never hold to the business," she says, "as hard as I hold to the people who are involved. I really hold to the people because without them there is nothing there."

"We were so close to making it happen, and it was really our dream idea. Now that dream idea doesn't matter so much," she says. "It was a dream working with this person."

The rules for how married people should get divorced are pretty well defined in our society. You file legal papers for a divorce and split things up according to some predetermined legal rules. By contrast, the mechanism for splitting up businesses is often not well-thought-out. An agreement should discuss what happens if sometime in the life of the business the interests of the partners diverge. Make a shareholders agreement that states all these things and have an attorney review it.

Future partners may balk at the idea of spending money so early on to draw up legal paperwork. They reason that they will always "be friends" and such a conflict could never arise between them. They laugh, nod, and smile at each other. Unfortunately, many times, years later, they are sitting across a different table with lawyers on each side yelling obscenities and accusations at each other. No written document is there to guide these "discussions." If you take only one piece of advice from this part of the book, take this one: Hire a lawyer and get a written agreement with your partner on how to divide up the business if you have irreconcilable differences.

The most critical point to resolve involves having a single partner. With a 50-50 split in voting rights, there must be a tiebreaker. What happens when the two of you simply can't agree on how to keep the business operation going forward? Talk to your attorney about including a "Texas Draw" provision in your partnership agreement. This is where one partner offers to buy out the other partner. The partner who has received the offer then has the choice of either taking the buyout offer or buying the other partner out for the same price. This ensures fair offers by both partners. Without a way for partners to resolve their differences, principals can get locked in a death spiral that may result in the demise of the entire company. Other things to put in your agreement include what happens to the business if one partner dies, becomes disabled, or gets divorced. Do you really want to be partners with the spouse of your partner? Key-man insurance can come in handy here as well.

This may all seem silly at the beginning, especially when you and your partner are "just married and in the honeymoon phase." But I guarantee that all this will matter if someday someone offers you millions to buy your company. The decisions are a lot easier to make when the company is starting out, and it is worth nothing rather than when there is a lot on the line. When my partner and I sold our business, we read through every word of the shareholders agreement many times. It guided us in our decision-making process. More important, it can help guide your daily conduct with each other and will really prevent the kinds of deadlocks that can end up being death spirals over a longer period of time.

Figure Out How You Will Divorce When You Get Married

J o d i T u r e k

Jodi Turek says the best lessons she learned about running a business she learned from watching her parents run their bagel shop. For the past four years, she has been busy imposing this common sensibility on a different type of enterprise altogether, the e-business Womensforum.com.

Turek launched WomensForum.com a couple of days after first going online. She saw the great sites being run by women, and she just had to pull their energies together.

Her business partner also happened to be her fiance. But the stress of merging business with relationship proved too much for either one of them, and they called the marriage off.

"I never thought of leaving the business," she says. "There were days that I shut my door and cried. Sometimes you could catch me facedown in the Ben & Jerry's. Your body will catch up with you.

"I was so proud of what we had built, there were other people who were dependant on us," she says. "It is kind of like having baby. You can't abandon it. It gets difficult. The thought of leaving the business never occurred to me."

WHEN PARTNERS WAR

Unfortunately, many times partners do not heed their advisors and do not structure their businesses correctly. What started off as a promising partnership has degraded into what can only be described as a mess.

One telltale sign is the absence of verbal communication between the partners. When it's degraded to this point, what follows is self-fulfilling assumptions on the part of each partner about the other's actions and behavior. Unfortunately, their destinies are legally bound together inside the business, preventing them from logically or civilly figuring out how to part ways.

This is when the partners go to war.

This sometimes starts out of simple desperation and frustration. Many times it ends in vengeance. I have been involved in war among partners that has been conducted through legal, physical, and psychological tactics. It is a horrible thing to participate in. It is even more difficult to witness people trying to destroy each other. As one of the combatants, you will stop sleeping and may even get sick. It can be debilitating. Your day and night dreams will be filled with awful scenarios. You will rerun moments with your partner through your brain constantly. It is no way to live. When my two partners kicked me out of my second business, I was sick in bed for a week from the physical and emotional strain.

C r e a t e   a   L e g a l   W a y   t o   B r e a k   t h e   C h a i n s

EXIT THE WAR—QUICKLY!

If you find yourself at war, look for a quick, reasonable, and fair resolution to the situation. Exit! Do not prolong your personal suffering or the pain of noncombatant employees who may be caught in your war. Whatever you think you may gain by battling your partner down to the end over an extended period of time is a delusion. Balance the legal advice that you receive with advice from your mentors who have been there before.

Absolutely nothing can be gained by prolonging these kinds of partnership wars. Whatever you think you can gain monetarily will actually be less once you subtract legal fees. It will be even less when you subtract the physiological toll it will take on you. At this point, you will both end up losers no matter what the outcome. Seek a solution that fits both of you in the long run. End this as soon as possible. Learn what you can, consolidate your gains, and move on to your next venture. Get a financial settlement that will enable you to fight another day or launch another business if that is what you want to do. Remember, it's not that winners never quit. Rather, it's all winners know how and when to quit. It's OK to leave the battlefield and lick your wounds. I assure you that your wounds, just like mine, will heal in time.

*A l l   W i n n e r s   K n o w   H o w
and   W h e n   t o   Q u i t*

A T r u e   T a l e
JONATHAN GINSBURG
The Searing Pain of Success

Jonathan Ginsburg and Elyse Seabart (not their real names) founded their company as 50-50 partners. The two worked on the company part-time for the first two years and then they went full-time.

Lots of folks thought the timing was off, but the partners thought the timing was perfect to gobble up the remains of a lot of companies in their industry.

It was, as Ginsburg says, one of those "what-do-you-want-to-do-in-life kind of deals." Both partners sensed change blowing in, so they both reorganized their lives around running their company full-time.

"E-commerce won't go away. All these people will need is a Web site," Ginsburg says. "It's the one fundamental anchor that people need. It's like electricity. It's part of being in the business these days.

"The goal was to put together a business to take advantage of that downturn," Ginsburg says. " We realized we had a pretty good opportunity in Web hosting. We already had customers, we had revenues, etc., and we had full-time jobs," Ginsburg says. "We decided to quit our full-time jobs because [of] the soon-to-explode dot-com bomb. When those things explode and you're rebuilding . . . they're services that people need, but the people providing them are just going to implode. They were built to scales that weren't sustainable."

With years of mergers and acquisitions experience gained working for the Big Six consulting firms, Ginsburg was the pure business-play guy, and Seabart, who had built the Web sites for Fortune 500 companies, was the techie. From the beginning, their company was a success.

"It's unbelievable," Ginsburg says. "Everybody thinks we're nuts for starting this business, and our monthly revenue goes up tenfold in the first 18 months. We didn't have business cards for six months, we've never advertised, nothing. It's all word-of-mouth referral, right? So everything is great."

Their company became known for good execution and business smarts. From all outward appearances, the business was doing very well. What nobody could see was that Ginsburg and Seabart were rapidly becoming the odd couple of entrepreneurs.

"I take Nexium every day for heartburn I never had until I started a business," Ginsburg says, "and I had a very stressful job before. But when you're right in the middle of it, it becomes really, really tough; and I think some of the big issues you have are what happens when you and your partner disagree.

"You're basically in a stalemate," Ginsburg says. "We were always great friends, we always saw eye to eye on things, and about six, seven months into the business, we found ourselves really not agreeing on how to get things done."

Ginsburg might say to Seabart about a product, "If you build it, they will come," while Seabart would reply by saying, "Show me the customers, and I will build it." It was an endless catch-22 with no resolution.

"You're in business because you absolutely respect each other," Ginsburg says. "You adore each other, you'd do anything for each other; but now you're married, you're living under the same roof, and all these little idiosyncrasies that you never really knew about before because you didn't have to live with the person 24 hours a day start driving you up a wall. So it's that first six months of marriage when you're ecstatic, but on the flip side, the person can drive you up a wall over nothing."

To grow the business, Ginsburg and Seabart were literally living with each other 24 hours a day. They were sharing a cheap apartment, not taking salaries, cutting corners, and committed to doing whatever it would take to make the business work. And, at home and at work, they were embroiled in a mini *War of the Roses*.

"Eight months into it, we're driving each other up a wall," Ginsburg says. "It's like a newly married couple realizing that this person hits the snooze 15 times, and I can't stand it. Would you just get out of bed and get up, or set your alarm an hour later!"

The partners trusted each other so implicitly that they hadn't sweated the start-up details. "We never put together those formal things [about] how to manage this business when we're successful," Ginsburg says. "And that created some tension."

Their communication styles were fundamentally different. Neither Ginsburg nor Seabart would speak up when they were truly upset. They had basic disagreements about how to proceed in specific areas of the business.

"Actually one of the best meetings we ever had," Ginsburg says, "is [when] there were a lot of really good, successful things going on, but there was a little bit of tension on how to do certain things or get things done, or what was the best way.

"We had a meeting with our business advisor and [Seabart] actually is a very low-key person. We were talking about something, and she got upset, and she kind of dropped her pen and said, 'No way. We're not doing it that way.'"

"I almost started laughing. I want to get her mad," Ginsburg says. "I'm like, 'This is great, absolutely great, because I knew you were upset about that, and you wouldn't say anything. I wasn't sure if I was doing something wrong, if you were upset, if you were thinking about something else. I couldn't figure out if you had something going on you weren't telling me. But I thought you were upset at me, and now I know.'"

This first true interaction in a long time helped clear the air between the two partners.

"I'm [thinking] now we can talk about this," Ginsburg says. "And she says, 'You're not upset that I'm upset about this?' I'm like, 'No. I just thought you were.' And our business advisor was saying 'Jeez, I feel like a marriage counselor.'"

Ginsburg says that was one of their first breakthroughs, when they learned to allow themselves to disagree with each other.

"An argument, by definition, has to do with some anger," Ginsburg says. "You can either use that energy positively or negatively. So I think that's another good thing, make sure you use that [energy] positively when you do disagree."

Another breakthrough was when the partners came to understand that they had been so worried about their joint creation falling apart that they wouldn't let anything go.

"The reality is that you've got to let some things go," Ginsburg says. "So what are the two things you can do really well? The things you can only do well enough, those are the same as doing them badly when you're starting a business, so just let it go and be OK with it."

And, finally, they came to understand that they were operating from fear rather than from a plan. Because they hadn't made a plan in the beginning, they were too often governed by their emotions. They were afraid of their plans not working, but even more than that they were afraid of letting each other down.

The partners now talk about what's going on. The "marriage counseling" has ended because they put together the structure to get together and talk about things.

"We literally get together once a week for an hour to talk business and to address any issues that are going on," Ginsburg says. "We had to learn it's OK to disagree. Nobody's going to go anywhere, nobody's going to quit, it's OK. We're in this together, and nobody's going away.

"The one thing that always holds things together is that ultimately we may disagree with each other on how to get somewhere, but we trust each other implicitly. And if you don't have that, you can just forget about it."

6

NETWORKING IS NOT A VERB

Take This Card and Shove It

BUSINESS AS RELATIONSHIPS, NOT RELATIONS

During more economically challenging times, the only competitive capital you have is your business relationships. Forget your company's intellectual property or your patents. It takes a lot of money that your business may never have to defend these against wealthy competitors. As an entrepreneur, your real competitive advantages are the trusted business relationships that you have developed with your team, customers, employees, and vendors. The management consulting group, Peppers and Rogers, calls this special status a *trusted agent*. For ten years, Don Peppers and Martha Rogers have focused on customer-based strategies. They invented the phrase *one to one* to highlight the importance of treating each client differently.

The famous business saying, "It's not what you know, it's who you know," is especially true now. *What you know* skills may qualify you to do a project. But you may never get invited to actually bid on it unless you have established the right relationships. You will never win if you are not allowed to play. And I don't mean this in the context of nepotism or unqualified companies getting business purely through favors or connections. I mean that it is important for companies to have an established track record with a customer. This is why it is especially difficult to replace an incumbent, a company that already has been doing similar work. It is far easier and less costly to get additional business from your existing customers than to find new ones. These relationships are a core asset of your business. Treat them that way.

Honor **T**hem

PEOPLE, NOT CAPITAL, ARE MY CURRENCY OF CHOICE

A main goal early in your business is to find customers who will trust you enough to give your young company a chance. They need to take a risk on you, although you may have little track record. You need to build trust capital.

For many established companies during the Internet bubble, it became fashionable to award business to young upstarts who were considered key to the New Economy. They were going to take your business in a new revolutionary direction. You just had to look at the rising Nasdaq stock exchange to convince yourself of this. Weren't these companies with little sales worth billions of dollars? Established companies reasoned that the market must know something. These managers were heroes for trying a new company because it showed that they could "think outside the box."

During this time, demand for products and services outstripped supply. The average salesperson needed to just sit by the phone, wait for it to ring, and take orders. Seemingly everyone was a star salesperson. But what we are learning in the 2000s is that we did not train salespeople in the later part of the 1990s; we trained order takers. Unfortunately, we paid them like they were salespeople.

We now find ourselves in a place where any business seeking a supplier for a given product or service has many choices. It's called competition! These options usually include, and place a high emphasis on, someone with whom it has an established relationship. Just as it is your friends and relatives who will give you capital to kick off your business, customers who know you and have an established relationship with you will take the risk and give you that first chance at doing business with them. While I admire people who are good cold callers and are able to find customers in this way, it is becoming a dead art in business today. This method of building your business makes customer acquisition expensive and time-consuming. While the cold caller may get in the door for an appointment and may even get to bid on the project, he or she is still sitting at "the kids' table" when all the important decisions are made on who will be awarded a project. The trusted agent, not you, will have the ear of the decision maker.

*P*eople *A*re *L*ike *G*old

YOUR NETWORK IS YOUR LIFE

Building a network of personal and business relationships is a life-long process. It really has no beginning and no end. In fact, some people do business because they went to kindergarten together! You only need to examine college alumni associations to understand how powerful these connections can be. The network of people you know socially or who do business with you is one of the most valuable assets you have to start a business. These may be the only people who will give you the chance you need. It amazes me that someone I knew ten years ago could become a great prospective client for me now.

The process of meeting new people and expanding your network takes effort and diligence. Everyone is not a prospective client. Networking as a verb should be eliminated from the English language. Building a personal network does not mean shoving your business card into my hand and asking me what I can do for you. It happens much more slowly and evolves in a different way if you are to be truly effective. When I get home, the business card that was shoved in my hand goes into the garbage. I am not really interested in remembering that person's name so I can do business with them in the future.

I methodically store in my PDA (Personal Digital Assistant, such as a PALM, Handspring, Pocket PC) the names of most new people I meet and how each connection was made. I record the e-mail, mobile, and home number of every person I meet. I try to stay in touch at least quarterly and see how I can make connections for them. E-mail and other forms of electronic communication in our world make this very easy to accomplish. Simultaneously, there is nothing wrong with asking these people to connect you with three people they know who might be interested in what you are doing. Use their good referral to get past a gatekeeper to the person you would like to contact. This strategy will give you a chance to tell your story 95 percent of the time. It will also enable you to grow your network over a long period of time. This is exactly one of the components you need to successfully grow your business.

Although contact information on the Web has made it easy to get in touch with people, the only surefire way to almost guarantee a contact is a referral. There is no substitute for a title line in the e-mail or an opening statement in a conversation that says: "Bill Gates referred me to you." Otherwise, your message may get mixed in with the other daily spam even if it reaches its intended destination. I have deleted messages from many people trying to get in touch with me because there was no referral in the subject line and I thought it was a spam e-mail selling ink cartridges!

When I first sold my company and wanted to build my business network in 2000, I was referred by an acquaintance to Steve Miller, founder of Origin Ventures. He was well-known in town as an intelligent and savvy angel investor. I was impressed when I heard him speak at a local business conference, and I wanted to meet him. I e-mailed him, and he agreed to meet with me at a local Starbucks although neither of us drink coffee. Our meeting lasted only 20 minutes, but it was very valuable to me. We have since become good friends. I was even able to "network" him with the woman that ended up being his wife! (I admit, I met my wife on a "networked" blind date too, and that introduction has lasted 15 years already!)

Steve also taught me that as I grew my network, I should never pass up an opportunity to meet with someone. You never know the role that person or a referral from him or her might play in your current or future business. It is often fun to play "geography" and figure out how you can help each other. I am constantly amazed at the connections that

L *iz* **R** *y a n*

"**N**etworking is about the person we are meeting. People have inherent value in and of themselves, and when we use people to accomplish our end, it's immoral."

"It's great to make relationships with people such that it enlarges the circle of people who are orientated toward helping each other. Networking is not about what we are promoting, rather it's networking about the person, networking about Jane and Allison and Sally and Julie Ann. Not networking about let me drive through Sally to get that which Sally has access to."

"Networking when it's about the person is wonderful and appropriate. It's a good thing that societal bonds have loosened and something in the culture has changed a bit so relative strangers feel free about contacting each other, and saying, 'Let's have lunch.' I love that. But if your sole purpose is specifically about business, gaining a financial end, it's gross, it's inappropriate, it's intrusive, it's calculating, and it's immoral."

"I went to a networking training I was invited to where the speaker said, 'Practice your pitch.' Then you walk up to somebody and you say, 'Here's my pitch.' It's like, well, why don't you just tattoo it on your freakin' forehead? What are we all, just billboards to go around and say, 'Here's what I do in my business, and here's what I need'? If somebody comes up to me and says, 'Here's my need,' I'm going to say, 'What made you think I wanted to know that?' I mean I'd be interested in meeting you and knowing you. But why would your need be a conversation starter?"

are made this way. Don't just do this for the business gain, do this to give back to all those people who have provided connections for you at one time or another.

In fact my writing this book in some ways evolved from having breakfast with Sally Duros, whom I had met at a networking event. Sally coached me and was the creative editor as I wrote this book. Having lunch with Jackie Huba, a local consultant and author, enabled me to meet with Jon Malysiak, acquisition editor at Dearborn Trade, which eventually published this book.

Y *our* **L** *ife* **C** *reates* **Y** *our* **N** *etwork*

DON'T RUSH TRUST

Building relationships, like building a business, takes time. Every business grows at its own pace, and so do associated business relationships. Be patient and don't push evolution. Don't rush trust. It is not based on how much you push someone or how much money you invest in trying to make a relationship work. It is about striving for Minimal Achievement as the Zen Buddhists say. Start small. I try to ask for very little from a newfound colleague in the first six months of meeting them. I do not believe in "trading" on new relationships too soon. That is, I don't ask my new relationships for anything. People are so used to being asked for favors that when you ask for nothing, they are surprised and grateful. Initially, it is important to give these people more than you get. Make connections for them. Find them new opportunities. This will build a much stronger and tighter bond over the long term. You will become that trusted agent for this person.

Not every day is a good day to network for an entrepreneur. Maybe you are too busy to pay attention to meeting new people, or you feel you are at the bottom of the roller coaster and are too depressed to form a good impression. This is exactly when you should go out and make new connections to help bring you out of your funk. If you feel desperate, slow down and focus. During these times, find one person new to meet or find a person you already know and add to the depth of your relationship. It will lift you up and give you the hope you need to get back into your car and journey again up the business mountain.

In any relationship, our impressions are formed very early on. It is very difficult to change this first impression. If you start off on a bad foot with someone, it is nearly impossible to recover for they will not give you a chance. They will view everything you do in a negative light. For them, you become a self-fulfilling prophecy of someone they don't want to be associated with. They will make you into the person they think you are. If you fall into the mud, it's hard to come out smelling like a rose.

Alternately, get off to a good start, and your relationship has unlimited opportunity to grow. Follow up on whatever you promise and appreciate anything you may get in return. Treat each relationship with special attention.

You will know that you have reached that glorious trusted agent status with someone when he or she refers business to you even when you have not requested it. The day that you hear, "Daniel at Pennewig Company referred me to you and said that you could do a good job," you should smile to yourself. You have arrived as a trusted agent.

B *ecome a* T *rusted* A *gent*

STARBUCKS IS SWITZERLAND

We use a lot of electronic gadgets today to communicate with each other. My cell phone is always on except when I am sleeping (this is a concession to my family). As I travel from meeting to meeting during the day, I receive and send e-mail through a wireless Handspring Treo PDA. Technology has made teleconferencing relatively inexpensive but still ineffective. For all this quick and easy communication, there is still nothing that replaces face-to-face meetings to build relationships with other businesspeople. We still board airplanes every day to travel to business meetings. As social beings, we still don't really solidify relationships until we meet someone in person. This enables us to complete our picture of him or her and move to the next step of the relationship.

Furthermore, we need to eat meals together to truly build on what we have started with another person. This tradition and importance of breaking bread has not really changed for thousands of years. It is popular to "do" lunch or breakfast.

We have slightly modified it for our purposes. Just as all business is no longer conducted in gray suits, white shirts, and red ties, businesspeople no longer just meet in offices and restaurants. We now meet for "coffee." In *Pour Your Heart into It,* Howard Schultz, the CEO of Starbucks, describes how he built the culture of this company to reflect his business establishment as a third place for people to meet. He states that the first place is your home. The second place is your office. He wanted to make Starbucks the third place to meet. I know he succeeded for I go to Starbucks for a lot of meetings, and I do not even drink coffee. But I do drive there in my 1963 Ford Falcon and black jeans to meet many entrepreneurs because few start-up businesses have office space that is more comfortable than Starbucks. It is always convenient (isn't there one on every corner?), conversation is friendly, and it has WI-FI Internet connections for my computer. I prefer these kinds of meetings because they seem much more personal and balanced than going to one or another's office, which may be cramped and less comfortable than Starbucks.

In the business world, Starbucks is Switzerland. It's neutral territory, which places a lot less stress on getting together or expectations for the meeting. Starbucks meetings can also be short. By definition, going for "coffee" is more than a phone conversation but less formal and requires less time then breakfast, lunch, or dinner (in that order). Dinner is typically reserved for special out-of-town guests or to celebrate signing a big deal. This casual atmosphere also enables businesspeople to get more quickly to the point for my average Starbucks coffee lasts 20 to 30 minutes. (That is how long it takes me to drink a bottle of water!) Like modern "gladiators," in this environment we can deal with each other face-to-face without hiding behind big desks or PowerPoint presentations. If there is a business connection for both, then a follow-up office meeting is a great next step! Maybe we can even "do lunch"?

We are all social beings, and we need these kinds of meetings for personal and professional growth. Additionally, when someone wants to network with you, he or she rarely forgets this kindness and appreciates your time. Even when I am very busy, I try never to turn down an opportunity to talk on the phone, or have breakfast, lunch, or coffee with someone. I have never regretted a single meeting I have had with anyone for I never know what path it will lead me and my business down.

Find Pleasure in Meeting New People

BUILD YOUR CURRENCY IN PEOPLE

Relationship currency with people is a fluid and an ever-changing commodity. Like the money currency markets, relationship currency has the potential every day to trade up or trade down beyond your control. Before I learned this, I thought that I could build a bank of chips—like in a game of poker—that I earned through my relationships with people and then cash them in with that person anytime I wanted. I was drastically disappointed when rules changed, and my chips became worthless. This can be an unfortunate consequence of this game that is much more art than science.

This can happen in many ways. People change jobs so your currency with them may become worthless (or it could become more valuable based on what company they join). One extremely bad incident in your relationship with the person could wipe out all your chips. Alternately, maybe the other person wasn't keeping score the same way you were and has you marked down for a lot less "relationship currency" than you think you have.

Don't take any of your relationships for granted for no one is truly beholden to you. As in so many other parts of your business, learn to be humble. Think that you have less rather than more currency with someone. This is why it is so important to keep your relationship capital with a person fresh through current contacts with them. If a relationship is not building or growing, then it is probably fading. Accept this, and move to form a new relationship in the same company if that is what your business needs.

Relationships Have to Be Tended

"I make introductions to people I meet who I think would have synergies together, whether or not it has any business advantage to me."

"I believe that when you're building community, people eventually refer business back to you; I think that's how I get a lot of business. Eventually, people know what you do. You've been helpful to them, so it's just at the top of that person's mind. I've been doing that for years, ever since I've been in technology."

Stephanie Covall-Pinnix

GROW YOUR RELATIONSHIPS

Ensure that your most important relationships continue to grow. Even if infrequent, relevant e-mails, referrals, and updates are all good ways to accomplish this. I detest blanket newsletter updates to everyone in a person's database. While this may be a good way for businesses to keep each other up-to-date, this is too impersonal for individuals. Spend time at least quarterly to think about how you build your relationships with people through relevant contact. I typically look at my entire contact list every few months and pick out people that I have not talked to or met with in a while. It is very effective.

It is important that after six months of building your capital with someone that you test what you have. Ask him to do a very small favor. Ask him to make a connection for you with someone he knows. A single phone call will do. Evaluate the results and adjust your "currency bank" with this person accordingly.

Alternately, some people are really bad at this. They are wacky or inexperienced. This is why, as an entrepreneur, it is your responsibility to manage the relationship to meet your personal or business goals. Don't depend on others to do it for you. This is not the same thing as seeking to control the relationship. Rather, it is about taking the initiative to get what you want out of it.

It may also be difficult to reconnect with people who you have fallen out of touch with for a long time. People always appreciate a "long time no see" call or e-mail. You will be surprised, if there was a relationship at one point in time, to see how easy it will be to get reconnected. If you would like to reconnect with someone who was involved with you in a failed business relationship, approach her with honesty and humility. Don't be embarrassed. People will accept this and may even want to renew the relationship even if their first attempt with you was a failure. Most business relationships have redeeming value. If your call or e-mail goes unanswered over a period of time, you know that you no longer have relationship capital with that person.

You may not always get "the credit" for linking up two people for a successful business relationship. Alternately, you will probably always hear about it if it fails. Don't be discouraged. Even if you do not get thanked, you can circle back to both people individually and ask how it went. This will accomplish the same gaining of relationship capital and you will still be able to build on it.

At the same time, extracting value for making a connection should not be your primary concern. A prime motivator should not always be "What's in it for me?" Many times having your hand out can actually stifle a relationship before it even gets going. If you have made an effective connection between two people, then some benefit will ultimately come of it. Even if you do not gain personally, you have helped create a culture for business to develop. Think of it as your contribution to a new ecosystem.

I do not mean to suggest that you should open up your entire contact list to everyone. I jealously guard my entire database of more than a thousand people I have personally met. If you are not careful, a bad referral to one of your contacts can mangle your relationship with that person. I typically only give out e-mail addresses and ask people for permission to refer. This provides another touch point with the person and becomes almost an opt-in, permission-based marketing system. The referred person knows an e-mail is coming. At the same time, you do not need to stay in the middle of the relationship of the people you connect. You will not have time for this, and there is no need to manage other people's relationships. Trust that they can take care of themselves. If they form a new relationship based on your introduction, this is good for you. Many times they will return the favor.

Grow **R**elationships with **I**ntegrity

CONNECT BUSINESSES WITHOUT USING THE LETTER "Z"

During the Internet bubble of the 1990s, many companies built incubators or tried to mimic the Japanese *zaibatsu*. In Japan, this "financial clique" was originally family controlled companies in banking and other industries. They were an essential and powerful part of Japan's economy for more than 100 years.

American incubators and Internet zaibatsus failed because they tried to create unnatural synergies that did not exist between businesses. I was never sure that sharing accounting departments, development staffs, or ad agencies really gave start-up businesses an advantage over their competition. Look at the former portfolios of bankrupt Divine Interventures and it will be difficult to assess how such a mass of diverse companies could be profitable together.

The z word always scared me. After I learned to pronounce it, it still sounded way too complex for any start-up business to handle. Ironically, I only later learned that zaibatsu sounds a lot like the Russian word *zaebatsya,* which translates to "overly fucked," or literally "to grow overly tired performing a certain task [or having a certain action performed to/on you]."

I bet some of the companies involved in the American zaibatsus during the past five years can relate to this.

Businesses should be brought together to do business not just to share resources or office space. The market will determine if the synergies are there or not. In the case of Divine Interventures, the market spoke. As previously stated, the company filed for bankruptcy in 2003, and the assets were sold.

Bring **B**usinesses **T**ogether to **D**o **B**usiness

FORM ALLIANCES THE NATURAL WAY

Businesses need to form natural alliances. Connections among businesses evolve and should not be forced. Sometimes company connections are simply multiple connections among many people in the two businesses. This can begin to involve a lot of personalities and thus get complicated. The best way to form connections between companies is not to emphasize the people but to transform the connection into needed products or services.

Start doing a small piece of business together. This is a good test case for every business relationship solidifies with the payment of that first customer invoice. Also, it is not necessary to begin in the best place, but rather begin where the companies can help each other immediately. Each successful completed project will form new bonds that will transcend the personalities of the people involved in the company. As an entrepreneur, this is what you want because people come and go in companies. When your connection leaves, you want to be able to point to all the business you have conducted with that company as a tie that will bind you. There is nothing that is stronger for solidifying relationships.

Create a **B**ond **T**hat **L**asts

A True Tale

MARSHA MCVICKER

The Right Mentor at the Right Time

It was when Marsha McVicker's whizbang dot-com Errand Solutions was experiencing its worst crisis that McVicker discovered how many friends she truly had.

"By August 2001," she says, "everything in the business was falling apart—personally and professionally.

"We weren't anywhere close to being profitable," she says. "My office in Chicago was broken into, all of our computers were stolen, the server, everything! I lost all my data, all my contact lists, everything was just wiped out.

"Then our phones didn't work for a week," she says. "We had no new business coming in the door at all. I had no idea how I was going to make payroll. I had $4,000 in the bank, and I had a burn rate of about $40,000. I was in serious, serious trouble.

"We were like OK—what should we tackle first? It was so overwhelming," she says. "We couldn't take incoming calls for a week. That did not deter us from making outgoing cell calls for money and sales."

Finally, she called a "Come to Jesus" meeting with her staff, where she opened the books and told them where everything was at.

"Failure is not an option," she says. "Entrepreneurs are inherently overly optimistic. We are very skewed in our vision of the future. When you are scraping the bottom, there is nowhere except up to go.

"I was fortunate in that I had an incredible network of family, friends, and supporters," she says. The period to come was rough. McVicker says she did not pay herself for two years.

But there was one man—and McVicker's voice catches as she talks about him—whose personal support had helped her at the start and sustained her at key moments as she rebuilt after everything around her had crumbled. His name was Bob Zobel.

Errand Solutions calls itself an errand and convenience service. The initial target customers were corporations who would provide Errand Solutions services as part of a benefits package to attract and retain employees.

In 1999, McVicker was planning to dominate the world with the first e-commerce company in Wisconsin. She was working on her supply-chain management MBA from the University of Wisconsin in Madison when she won a business-plan competition and a sizable cash prize.

"I had won the $100,000. I was talking on the phone to my parents and I was screaming, 'Now I really have to start this. This is so fantastic,'" she says. "Bob Zobel was overhearing my telephone conversation, and he said to me, 'You can come and have one of my offices.'

"I cannot tell you how this man totally guided the development of Errand Solutions," she says.

"He gave me my own private office," she says. "He would come in regularly and ask 'How's it going? What are you struggling with today?'"

McVicker first met Zobel—who was head of the Facilitator Capital Fund, which invested in predominantly old-school businesses—during those still halcyon days of 1999. McVicker had been able to leverage that first $100,000 prize into a technology development loan from the U.S. Department of Commerce. The prize and the loans were like honey to angel investors, and over the life of the business, she was able to raise more than $3 million from them to get her e-commerce site launched and her business running.

She signed on her first client, Kraft Foods, in March 2000. That's when she learned that 97 percent of her clients would prefer interfacing with her company face-to-face. Scratch using the Web site for transactions.

Then came the crash of the Nasdaq. Errand Solutions quickly dropped the dot.com from its name. The company struggled through its difficult start-up period until the problems converged into one big crisis around the time of the break-in.

When everything collapsed, everything also fell apart for McVicker. Her boyfriend of seven years broke up with her around the time of the "Jesus" meeting. And that's when McVicker stopped taking a salary. None of this was lost on Zobel.

"He would just write out a check," she says. "'Go buy yourself some groceries. Make sure that there's gas in the car. Or pay the rent.' He was like a grandfather to me and he was a mentor.

"My father scraped together as much cash as he could to keep me eating," she says. "My girlfriends were inviting me to dinner. You have no idea how much these simple things mean.

"There was a lot of luck and a lot of aligning of the stars to help me succeed," she says.

"Bob Zobel passed away last year," McVicker says. "He was 67. After I lost my mentor, the growth of my business did slow. Mentors are such powerful influences in young entrepreneurs' growth. I don't know if he ever realized how much he meant to me and the business. I can't advocate enough that seasoned entrepreneurs become mentors. It makes all the difference in the world—whether you succeed or don't.

"It wasn't just me [he mentored]," she says. "He did this for so many people. At his funeral, there was a line around the block just to get in the church. He had adopted an entire orphanage in Bolivia. We would all go down to Bolivia and help with this orphanage.

"Bob would always say 'You will be coming with me next year,'" she says, her voice catching. "I was unfortunately never able to go down. He had an incredible sense of humor. He was constantly giving and he had a great big heart.

"I try to emulate him in my life," she says. "My entire team knew how much he meant to me. We named the conference room, the Zobel room. Everybody was crying.

"He would never tell you what to do," she says. "He supported whatever choice you made. He would tell you stories about what he had seen happen in other people's lives.

"He was a true believer that you had to find your own way," she says.

"One of the common denominators for those of us who have companies is the mentor factor," she says. "You cannot do this alone. There is no way. You need a support network. I have been very fortunate. There are many people who have given generously in guiding the development of my business."

7

MY TRUTH ABOUT GETTING STARTED AND RUNNING A BUSINESS

Steady as She Goes

STARTING FROM WHERE YOU ARE

We all start businesses from different places in our personal lives based on our upbringing and past business experiences. Business mirrors the strengths and shortcomings of each person. Your business becomes the reflection of who you are. It is critical to understand that where you start from profoundly affects and shapes the character of your business. There are Five Fingers of Zen Buddhism. My favorite is the one that states, "Always start from where you are right now."

I have seen people start from many places. I started my three businesses at various points in my life, with different perspectives and motivations. All of these shaped what type of companies I started, whom I started them with, and what they became or did not become.

Know **W**here **Y**ou **A**re

DREAMING THE IMPOSSIBLE DREAM

When I started my first company, I wanted to create the perfect business I had read about in Paul Hawken's *Growing a Business* in 1988. Soon after finishing this book, I launched Lincoln Park Publishers on a part-time basis with my girlfriend (now my wife) and my best friend, Zane, and his wife. The company sold a guide listing all the types of places that delivered in Chicago. I prepared feverishly for its launch, diagramming every part of the operation. I built the business perfectly on paper and dreamed about how much fun it would be for all of us. Less than a year later, the business failed miserably as a result of my naïveté about running any type of business myself.

My dreaming blinded me from the fact that the business assumptions learned at a multibillion-dollar company such as IBM had no relationship to the challenges of a start-up. We ran out of cash. Employees would quit, and customers would not pay. I was shocked and disappointed. I did not know what hit me except I was now $5,000 poorer. This never happened at IBM! It took me a long time to figure out that my experience in a large business had very little to do with the skills I needed to run my own small business.

I also realized that it is nearly impossible to really make a business successful if you are only working on it part-time. It is a good idea to test the waters when you start a business by not quitting your day job. But at some point, you have to leap full-time into the new business to really make it work. Having a successful career at IBM, I was unwilling to do this in 1988.

It is very important to dream, but be prepared for the realities of running a business. Be prepared for a vision and set of expectations that can change almost daily. Look into your motivations to make sure that you really want to set out on this path. As with most things encountered in life, the dream of starting a business can be a lot more fun and glamorous than actually starting it.

But **L**ook **H**ard at **R**ealities

STARTING BY DOING GOOD

I also started my first business by wanting to do good in the world like Paul Hawken described. I longed to use my business skills for the betterment of the people around me. I am not the right kind of person to volunteer in a soup kitchen. But translating this sense of doing good into a business that can really make the difference can be a challenging task. The desire alone to build a profitable business that does good is nearly an impossible task. You need to find the business model that will yield the revenue or cash to actually create a company that does the good you target. Don't start without a solid plan or you will find yourself begging for donations and no track record of success.

Look to partner with organizations or individuals who are already in the place where your business wants to be. Maybe even go work for these organizations before you strike out on your own. This will give you a basic network for the industry, client contacts, and the ability to explore a model that may already be working. Take your time, and find the place where you can have maximum impact.

B *ut* P *lan for* R *evenue*

"Often I think that I am lucky to recognize that this is something that I wanted to do. It is that carpe diem. If you think this is what you want to do, don't waste any time; entrepreneurs know that they have only so much time. I haven't got much time to be here."

"There are different stages of life. If you are a person who is in touch with who you are and where you are—this is what matters to me and I am so crazy about it. If you look at it that way, success or failure doesn't matter."

"Part of the mentality of an entrepreneur is that you have never quite arrived. Entrepreneurs definitely have a save the world, fix the world complex. They want to help the world learn."

Suzi Bonk

GOING IT ALONE

When I joined two other guys to start my second business, I had just been fired from my job at Whittman-Hart. I had left IBM to strike out into the business world and work for a smaller company. Now I was eager to take it all the way on a full-time basis and start my own business.

I started from the place of wanting to go it alone. At this point in my life, I didn't care what other people thought, and I wanted to pursue my own ideas with conviction. I was finished working for someone else, and I wanted to show the world that I could build my own company. I was done with tying my business future to a boss. I was so eager to strike out on my own that I started a business with the next two guys that came through the door (I found them in the classified section of a local newspaper). Again, I fell flat on my face because I was excited about the business idea but knew nothing about the people with whom I was forming a company. I thought I could single-handedly make the business successful despite my partners. I was wrong about everything.

The part of anyone that wants to go it alone fits well into the entrepreneurship lifestyle. Sometimes you need to say "To heck with the rest of the world" and put your head down to follow your own vision. Many times, this is what it takes to get a business off the ground. But somewhere in the progress of creating or building your business, you need to find other "lunatics like you" who can help you build the company. You need to build a team of people and add vendors to complement yourself.

Is *a* **B***eginning* **B***ut* **N***ot an* **E***nd*

STARTING AS A CONSULTANT

Before starting my second business, I had worked mostly in a consulting capacity at IBM and Whittman-Hart.

After doing this for a while, I wanted to try and work for myself. This is a very difficult transition to make. A person who has only worked for a Big Six consulting firm backed up by that logo on his business card really has no idea what it is like to work for his own company. My own transition from working for IBM and then starting a small business made me feel like I had been flown to a planet where businesspeople spoke a different language. Initially, no one returned my phone calls or was interested in what I was selling. This confused me because my product was similar to what I had handled at the larger company. I soon realized why people returned my sales calls at my former employer. As I indicated, it had less to do with me and more to do with the fact I represented IBM.

Advising other owners on their business as a consultant and then leaving them to execute on your advice is very different from what an entrepreneur does. The business owner weighs the advice provided by many sources and its possible outcomes, and makes a decision. Then he waits for the results. Unlike the consultant, he doesn't get to send a bill and go home at 5 PM. The entrepreneur doesn't get paid unless his decision is successful.

Before venturing directly from a large consulting business to your own venture, I suggest you work at a "halfway house." Go work for someone in a 15- to 30-person company to see what it is really like. Whittman-Hart provided this transition for me from IBM. You will learn a lot from the owner of the business and at the same time provide yourself with a safety net. You will also appreciate the security.

G*et* E*xperience* F*irst*

> "Successful entrepreneurs are willing to leave. They're willing to abandon credibility, security, name recognition, title, power, budget, heft, clout, influence, whatever you want to call it, by leaving a corporate job and putting on a name tag that says, 'XYZ Industries,' that no one has ever heard of."
>
> **Liz Ryan**

LANDING BY ACCIDENT

I began my third business simply to survive and support my family. Times were tough and I could not find a job. I did not necessarily strike out on my own the third time after failing on two previous attempts so that I could once again be an entrepreneur. Instead it was out of necessity. A friend of mine asked me to start a business with him. I saw no other options for making a living during the early-1990s recession, so I said yes. Under these circumstances, I was the classical entrepreneur, fitting the model of how businesses have been started for thousands of years. For all of time, people have started business out of necessity.

If you find yourself in this place, it is mostly a good thing. You may enjoy being "the Accidental CEO" as Manish Patel from Where2GetIt calls himself. But it is necessary to step back after a while and assess what you have achieved and who you are in business with. Decide whether you want or can continue to grow your business. It is also possible to now go to a similar company that would readily employ you for you can bring a book of business with you. Paying customers of your own always give you choices.

Is **Y**our **D**esire to **R**eally
Grow a **B**usiness?

COOL IDEAS DON'T ALWAYS
MEAN A BUSINESS

I also started my second business because I thought the technology we were selling was really cool. I was awed at the fact that in 1991 you could talk to a computer and it could "understand" what you were saying. I reasoned that "voice-activated computing" was the new "new" thing. In this case, most people I demonstrated the technology to were awed by it. They wanted to invest in the company. But at the same time, most of them would not buy it for their own companies for they could not justify its cost. They ultimately could not make the paradigm shift necessary to go from their current and reliable bar-code technology to voice-activated computing.

Many people create cool technologies. It's difficult, however, to find the business application for the many technical discoveries that we find every day at our universities and national laboratories. At these institutions, technology transfer is so difficult precisely because every "thing" that is created does not have commercial or moneymaking applications. The key is to find a problem that this "creation" will solve and get people to pay money for the solution. This is the first step in transforming a discovery into a profit-making venture. Finding that first customer who can use your creation is your first milestone. If you are successful with one, there's a good chance other customers or new applications can follow.

G *et* B *usiness* H *elp*

YOU WON'T FIND THE NEXT BIG THING IN THE PRESS

It is difficult to hit a moving target. Many people ask me what the next hot sector would be. As an angel investor and experienced entrepreneur, I always answer that I have no idea. Furthermore, it does not matter to me. Don't leap into a sector because it's hot. Go there because you know something about it. Go there because you see a problem that is not being solved. Go there because you know people in that sector you will enjoy working with. You will almost never hit the timing right unless you are lucky.

Unfortunately, business ideas are developed in packs. Many times people follow the headlines and try to spot that next trend. If you are looking in the press for the hot trend of the day, you have surely missed it. You need to look where no one else is looking. Although, if you find yourself the first and only one there, I would worry that there is no business and no problem. Most start-up businesses do not have the financial resources to be a "first mover." Don't get caught up in abstract ideas or exciting solutions looking for a problem. Don't try to follow the money. Go out and find pain points for prospective customers that they will pay money to fix. Business vitamins are a tough sell. The market for business painkillers is always open and often very profitable.

Business plans, as I read them, often come in clusters of ideas. It feels like déjà vu when in the course of a month, I read five plans on software for digital-asset management. I remember sitting in an angel presentation in 2000 where an entrepreneur was discussing his idea of putting pet events on the Web. Another angel leaned over to me and said, "This is the third business of this type I have seen this month!" For a while, everyone wanted to start a wireless business. It now seems that everyone wants to get into the nanotechnology business.

Whatever business you start should emerge organically from interests inside of yourself. You are missing the driving force of being an entrepreneur if you are looking outside yourself in the newspaper for the next killer application. I remember in 1989, a few of us wanted to get together and leave IBM and start our own business. We brainstormed a few times about what we should do but nothing ever emerged because there was no area of interest that we could all be passionate about. We ended up all leaving IBM but going our separate ways.

The **N**ext **B**ig **T**hing **I**s **Y**ours

THERE IS NO PERFECT TIME

Forget trying to pick the perfect time to launch the business you have been thinking about for months or years. There is no perfect timing or ideal situation. No amount of spreadsheet calculations or marketing research will finally convince you to go for it. Somewhere along the way you need to simply close your eyes and take that leap of faith and jump. If you are ready, people and circumstances have a way of choosing you. You will simply find yourself there. This is why more businesses are started during recessionary times of high unemployment. People find themselves without work, and the timing is right to start their own business because they are unable to find anything else to do. Being bored and having to pay your bills are a powerful combination for any would-be entrepreneur.

When I was kicked out of my second business, my first son was two months from being born. This was the definition of bad timing for sure. I didn't want to leave my last company but my two other partners gave me no choice with their swift "good-bye." A month later, when a friend of mine approached me to start a new business with him, I realized this was not a good time. Starting a business a month before your child is born is not something you would choose. Bringing a baby into your family requires a lot of energy and little sleep. Furthermore, in our new business, there was no promise of getting paid until at least six months after we started. This was not exactly a good way to start my life as a father and become head of a household. But I didn't want to turn down an opportunity to start a new business with someone I respected and enjoyed working with. We moved into our new office to set up the business a few weeks after my first son was born.

If you are unable to take the leap to start your business now, it's OK. View it as a signal that you are not ready, and be happy staying where you are for the present. You may be ready in another month or in another year. You may be ready when a totally different opportunity presents itself with different people. You may never be ready. It is important to remember that being an entrepreneur is not for everyone. In fact, it is the right choice for very few people. Entrepreneurship must choose you. Most people choose this path because they have to, not because they want to.

*S t a r t i n g   a   **B** u s i n e s s   **I** s   **N** o t   f o r   **E** v e r y o n e*

"A" DRIVERS AND "B" IDEAS BUILD BUSINESSES

I remember in the early 1990s, after two failed businesses, my father begged me not to start another business. With my wife pregnant with my first child, he told me what a horrible idea my new business was. He told me that customers would never buy our products (luckily he was wrong this time). What I learned from my previous failed business attempts was that the idea for this business was no worse than the ideas from the previous two. The difference was that with added years of experience and a great partner, I was able to execute it this time.

Anyone can have a great idea. But having that idea and executing that idea successfully are two different things. Execution is probably one of the biggest competitive advantages typically overlooked by businesses. Investors would always rather have an A driver with a B idea, then a B driver with an A idea. This is why angels and venture capitalists always rate the management team as the key criteria for deciding their investments. Ideas don't make profitable businesses. Management teams that successfully execute ideas make money.

A great example in American business of not having a unique business product but having superior execution is Microsoft DOS and Windows operating systems. Many of the ideas of the mouse and graphical interface for Windows did not originate with Bill Gates and Microsoft. Many would argue that Gates got these ideas from his competitors. What he did better than anyone else was execute a superior marketing and distribution strategy. More than ten years ago, Gates went to major computer manufacturers and negotiated a deal to put the Windows operating system on every computer they sold. This perfectly executed strategy made Windows the de facto operating system on the personal computer in the world. As a result, I believe that Gates's superior execution strategy, not his product line, is responsible for his dominant market share.

Outside of the technology world, the concept of a discount airline has been around for a long time. It is a current topic of conversation in a struggling industry. Major airlines such as United and American have tried to execute it many times. Only Herb Kelleher at Southwest Airlines has figured out how to make a low-cost point-to-point airline profitable. The idea is not unique but the successful execution is.

Execution Makes the Money

"Many do not make it. Those who do are entrepreneurial and enjoy the notion of starting at zero every month. Execution is really the differentiation between being successful and not. It is not white boarding. And [not] talking about what you want to happen."

John Banta

YOU HAVE NO IDEA!

A business idea is just an idea. It's simply words on a page. It's only the beginning of something. It's far too theoretical for me and does not represent a real business. You and I can sit and discuss the merits of a business idea all day. It's academic. Only when you go out there and execute and then ask the customer to buy your product do you have a real business. Additionally, only through execution will your business be truly born, evolve, and grow. Execution of your idea forces you as the leader to learn what the customer likes and dislikes. Execution enables the market to determine whether your idea put into action is a success or failure. If at first you do not succeed, you are able to "morph" or change your business into something that can give you another chance of success. I always urge people to "Do something, do anything." Use action to pick any path.

So, you have an idea for a new business or an idea for your existing business. Will it be successful? Admit that you really have no idea. Go out and try it. Your customers will buy it not because it is a good idea, but because you executed well. And that's what really counts.

And Neither Does Anyone Else

IT'S NOT IN MY JOB DESCRIPTION

Starting a business takes a lot of hard work. It is supposed to be hard. Daily tasks of hiring people, running payroll, keeping computer systems working, and taking out the garbage compete with the actual activity of the business. You may think that all these daily tasks interfere with why you actually got into the business. I remember in my last business how I had to spend a whole day at the Chicago City Department of Streets and Sanitation to answer a ticket charging that we had too much garbage in our outside disposal and it was causing a "neighborhood nuisance." I don't seem to remember allocating time for this activity in the business plan!

The vision in your mind of doing something is often different from the reality of doing it. The road of starting and running a business is littered with surprises. You are likely to repeat to yourself many times the phrase, "I never thought I would have to do that." Most entrepreneurs believe if they could only focus on the core of running the business, the journey would be a lot easier. If they could only make food for a restaurant or sell their product to customers who want it, things would be great. Unfortunately, this is not the case. Your business plan will never include what you will do when the computer network goes down, or where to find time to do the payroll taxes, or how to file sales taxes. Where do you write in your plan about waiting at an unemployment or equal opportunity hearing? Or how can you build your business if one of your best customers was just indicted by the Securities and Exchange Commission and they want your company to testify? Regardless of the result, you'll probably lose your customer. You may get angry. You may say that all these distractions are keeping you from doing the "real business" of your company.

I always felt that the word *entrepreneur* sounded too glamorous for what people do when they start a business until I found the linguistic origin of the world. Entrepreneur comes from the French word *entreprendre,* which simply means "to undertake." The *American Heritage Dictionary* defines it as "A person who organizes, operates, and assumes the risk for a business venture." I now think that the word pretty much covers it. You need to do it all. You need to organize the business, operate the business, and assume all the risk for the business. Doesn't this sound like fun?

Remember, it is all your job. As an entrepreneur, you are never "too good" to do any task for your company. Never. This is yet another lesson in humility learned by running your own business.

It's time to check the manual. All these things you call distractions don't get in the way. All these are part of the real business. This is one of the reasons it is so hard. This is why there is no such thing as a perfect plan for an entrepreneurial business. Certainly, early on, you cannot hire people to take care of things for you. Everything you label as a "distraction" is as much a part of your job description as is selling to customers, ordering inventory, and providing financial statements.

When I started my first business, I never thought I would have to clean the bathrooms or haul heavy bags of the next direct mail piece to the post office in the trunk of my car.

You are the owner. In the beginning, until you can afford other people, you are responsible for every need your business has.

Coming to this realization is not unlike being first exposed to the needs of newborn infants. When we had my first son I remember being surprised at how ill-prepared I was even though I had read every book on the subject, and my wife and I had "trained" at classes together. On a daily basis, I had no idea what would come next.

I remember thinking how shocked I was that the human race had continued to survive under these kinds of conditions. Furthermore, there were nights as a brand-new parent that I amused myself by empathizing with the animal kingdom where some species "eat their young"! I never imaged that having a child would be so all encompassing and exhausting. I never realized how it would touch and change every aspect of my life. There were times during those first few months after my son was born, when I really did wonder what I had gotten myself into with a baby in the house.

As in business, the only thing I could expect is what I never expected. Sometimes, I also wondered what was I thinking and how did I get here.

This business is your baby for you to care for and feed regardless of what happens. The sooner you realize this, the less time you will spend blaming other things for getting in your way. Remember that all these things are part of the way. They are part of a journey that has no road map and you will have to find your own path. Make it up as you go along like I did. Improvisation became one of my favorite words.

E*verything* I*s* Y*our* J*ob*

YOUR START-UP WILL BRING OUT YOUR BEST AND WORST

Running a business will bring out the best and the worst of who you are. It will bring out the best and the worst of whom you hope to be and the best and the worst of whom you are afraid to be. This happens because you will face a daily dose of extreme business situations that will stretch you in every way to the limit. The highest highs and the lowest lows possible will be part of your daily business life. It will be only natural for you to be happy and almost giddy when things are going well in your business and you are riding the growth curve. Sales and cash are coming through the door to feed your business. The best of you will praise people regularly, laugh with your customers, and forgive mistakes easily. Euphoria will dominate your every thought, and you will celebrate the day you dreamed this business up. The worst of you will think that you are King Midas and congratulate yourself alone for having achieved such wild and unprecedented success.

I guarantee things will change.

Perhaps the very next day, clouds will gather and a storm will roll in. Customers will not buy, no one will pay their bills, and your key employee will quit. The worst of you will loudly blame this on everyone around you and start a wild witch-hunt for a scapegoat. You may even fire someone just to make yourself feel better. You may even cry in despair and want to give up. The best of you will dig down for your passion and move past this temporary setback. You will remember the good days and why you are doing this in the first place. You will look for ways to turn the situation around.

As the leader, your attitude will affect everyone at your business. Good mood or bad mood, everyone will feel it. Many will even wonder if it is their fault. The back-and-forth can give your company whiplash. You do not need to always be positive or upbeat. This is unrealistic. Be honest about this. Admit when you are high or low. Communicate good or bad news to your other team members quickly and honestly.

Your Trickle-Down Emotions
Will Affect Everyone

STEP OUTSIDE, WATCH YOURSELF, AND LEARN

You may become so frenzied in your actions and thoughts that you may think you have become manic. Certainly, this is a feeling I had frequently running my own businesses. I questioned, sometimes daily, my psychological and physical well-being during my business journeys. Forgive yourself and hang on. We all go through this. Use it as a time to discover the limits of your own working style. What you learn about yourself and how you work during the good and bad times will be valuable information that you will be able to use as you grow your business. Forget about taking a Myers-Briggs test. Those results are worthless.

During these extreme times, you will find your true strengths and weaknesses as they relate to your business. You may want to write things down in a journal so you can reflect on them later. You can also keep notes in your PDA or on your computer. Date all your notes so you have a reference point when you review them. In your more contemplative moments, you will be able to reflect on patterns and sense what you have learned.

As a result, you will need to find people to join your team who can boost these strengths and compensate for your weaknesses. Initially, it will be difficult to find where you are strong or weak. Above all, it will be challenging to admit your limitations to yourself for, up to a certain point, you will be doing the entire business on your own. You can't admit that you do not know how to do something. Only more time and experience will help you here. A good team will not prevent the next storms from rolling in, but it will add ballast to stabilize your boat (and your well-being) when they do.

S t a b i l i z e   Y o u r s e l f   w i t h   t h e   R i g h t   P e o p l e

MIND YOUR BUSINESS

I have found that there is no better way to practice the Zen Buddhism philosophy of mindfulness than to run your own business. To be effective, you will have no choice but to be present here, today, right now.

I always struggled with being effective with the task at hand until I learned a favorite Zen Buddhist parable where two monks are discussing their Zen masters. One monk says to the other, "My master is so powerful he can walk across the water of this river without using a bridge." The other monk replies, "That's nothing. My master is so powerful that when he chops wood, he chops wood. When he cooks rice, he cooks rice."

The way I interpret this parable is that there is nothing more powerful in this world than just focusing on what you are doing right now. This taught me to focus on today. Mind your business. Deal with whatever your company throws at you right here right now. If you worry or focus on something like selling your business that may never happen, you will have a difficult time surviving today. You may even become frantic with all the variables you need to deal with over a month's time. Singular focus is hard, but it will help you through.

In this early stage, Matt McCall of Portage Venture Partners states there must be a balance between "experimentation with business models and focusing on specific market segments and customer needs." He believes that most firms early on "throw spaghetti up on the wall" to define which customers and products have the most potential. McCall sees a typical catch-22 for "until you begin to focus on a clear set of customer needs with an appropriate offering, you do not have a viable business."

O*ne* S*ingular* S*ensation*

FOCUS ON YOUR BUSINESS HERE AND NOW

Focus on building a business one customer at a time before you begin to think about exiting it or about how much someone might pay for it. Stop thinking about what you might sell the business for one day and just build it. Selling your business needs to be an outcome of the value you have built in your company not a goal in itself. If you build something of value, I guarantee someone will come to buy it one day if that is what you want.

If you start out with the objective of selling your business, you may even flip during these difficult times and instead ask yourself, "How do I just get out without losing everything I own?" Many times I said if I could just walk away from my business that would be OK. It was like I was in that 1963 Broadway play, *Stop the World: I Want to Get Off.*

Real business value is measured by cash flow and profits and your experience accomplishing this. Value is built simply by completing the sales cycle. Attract customers, sell them a product, and have them pay you for that product. This is the real productive motion of business life. Love it or leave it. It is not market positioning, great logos, great advertising campaigns, or large office spaces. Loyal and satisfied customers will attract corporate buyers of businesses.

If you build to sell, you will never build anything of value, and you will never sell your business for a substantial profit. Place your attention and intention in the present. If you build a business that has value, a buyer will someday come to your door and offer to buy your company.

If your passion is on some future goal without achieving the cornerstones of what is in front of you, you will not go far. If your only commitment is to a future exit strategy, how do you handle all the ups and downs that will come your way? The future will seem too remote and you will not be able to draw on that kind of distant goal to get you through anything.

An entrepreneur needs to be committed to his or her business right here, right now, in the present moment. Focus your mind on the next tasks that are directly in front of you. Your business will have no future if you do not solve issues today and accomplish your immediate goals. These may include many of the rudimentary things such as closing the sale on that next customer, hiring a new employee, or getting your computer system to work again. These tactical issues will require a lot of personal and focused energy. There is little glamour here for the entrepreneur, but these are your steppingstones to whatever the business will throw at you tomorrow or next month.

B *uild* **V** *alue* **D** *ay by* **D** *ay*

READ THE SIGN! SPEED KILLS

Every business has cycles. If you solve a problem for a customer and he or she pays you for it, this enables your business to eventually grow. But unlike what we heard in the 1990s, the natural course of business is to grow slowly over a long period of time. Be a patient entrepreneur. Change and growth in the best businesses happens slowly and incrementally. The push toward skyrocketing sales and growth usually leads to problems.

In the 2000s like in every other decade in American business except the 1990s, we will be building businesses piece by piece.

This incremental building process in the 1990s was replaced by a need for speed. Many business advocates insisted that the Internet changed everything. As a result we needed to work with increased speed 24 hours a day. After the crash of March 2000, we learned that the Internet did not change business fundamentals.

If there is one thing that we should have learned in the 1990s, it is this: Speed kills. Companies were launching their massive marketing campaigns even before their products were for sale. Investors put money into business plans before the ink was dry. Due diligence was conducted on the back of a napkin. Without each business going through the necessary stages of business growth that form a strong base, it collapsed under the weight of all the capital pumped into it.

I met an entrepreneur who had a very successful home-automation business. He had been profitable for three years putting fancy stereo systems into 10,000-square-foot homes. He was thinking now about expanding his business. So he had this "hangover mind-set" from the 1990s that he needed to get $1 million of outside capital to open up five more branches of his business all at one time. I told him that this was the wrong strategy. First, no professional investor will give you a million dollars for your business so you are wasting your time. I advised him to open up one additional location from his retained earnings and see what it was like to operate one remote business location. Go slowly, test your assumptions, and make the second one successful before taking on a third location. He told me that he did not realize things could still be done in this way!

Sometimes growth in business is so incremental it may barely be noticeable: two steps forward and one step back. Again, can you ride it?

Stages of Growth Are Necessary

"I think there is a big problem, which I'll call the Herman Miller chair syndrome. [Having caught this] a lot of people from big corporations who still had that success drive and had that frustration became entrepreneurs, but they became entrepreneurs in an environment where there seemed to be plenty of money; what they got was a lot of really flashy furniture and cool-looking interiors and Herman Miller chairs and wireless laptops well before their time."

Bob Okabe

THEIR MONEY CAN MAKE YOU STUPID

I think you can be very aggressive in your business, but if you try to push it too hard, it falls apart. I talk to many businesses and ask the entrepreneur, If someone gave you a million dollars what the heck would you do with it? Having too much money is also detrimental to starting a business. Where did it really get us in the late 1990s when capital poured into anyone with a business plan? When people have too much money, sometimes they get stupid and lazy. They don't have to think about it or be creative because throwing money at a problem can solve it temporarily. These entrepreneurs think that if you need customers, then spend money on a big fancy marketing campaign or build the best product that has ever existed. Where did the $50M market branding campaign for Marchfirst in 2000 lead the company except into bankruptcy? Forget about building awareness and waiting to sell your product. Focus your resources and get customers!

Another example is a company at which I am chairman that wanted to attend two conferences that cost $1,500 each. They asked me if I thought we should go. Well, if we had a lot of money we'd simply go to the Web site, punch in our credit card numbers, and go. But because we didn't have a lot of money, I called up and asked the organizers if I could get a discount on the conference for we were a small start-up company. The result? One cut his price in half and the other one let the company go for free. A simple phone call saved thousands of dollars that could go toward something else. We were forced to become more resourceful because we didn't have the money.

Lean **T**imes **M**ake **Y**ou **M**ore **R**esourceful

DON'T GROW YOURSELF BROKE

Let the business grow at its own pace without unnatural acts. A very common cycle of business is that after some initial success, a business will "grow itself broke." It does take capital to grow your business. More sales may require more employees, more inventory, or bigger facilities. Even though your business may be profitable on a monthly basis, these investments may lead to a cash crunch. Make sure that you plan your cash-flow analysis so you can support these activities. Outside capital from your family or friends may be easier to get at this point based on your results. But the lack of planning here will mean another minefield that you can hit and yet another way you can go out of business. This way is especially heartbreaking because at one point in time, you had a profitable company.

J *a c k* **K** *r a f t*

"*T*here is a difference between being smart and bright. I always look for people who are bright. Bright people bring a level of flexibility and quickness. They have facile minds. You need to be very bright to be an idea person.

"Brights process and use information. People who are intelligent, people who spend all their time thinking aren't necessarily bright.

"Brights recognize the threads. It is pulling on the threads and recognizing that the thread is attached to something that allows [brights] to really shine.

"A good biz person will get the info but only enough info to make an accurate decision that is somewhat less than 100 percent. A bright person examines facts, and when you cross over at 60 percent then you make a decision.

"They see the threads. It's easy for anyone to cross over a sturdy bridge. I think people who gather research—and gather and gather— are building a very solid bridge to cross.

"Entrepreneurs will find a way to weave twigs and threads so they have just enough support to get across the gap.

"This brightness and the recognition of ideas goes to the ongoing management of business because an entrepreneur has to make lots of decisions about things that he or she is not an expert at.

"I have been lucky enough and successful enough to observe [brights]. I love hanging around with these kind of people. Life is wonderful if you can surround yourself with them. And, oh, guess what? They bring opportunities to you."

The most difficult time to focus for many businesspeople is after your company has enjoyed a lot of success. After you have been profitable building the business at an early stage, you start to feel like you can do anything. You may even want to change your name to King Midas because you may feel you have that magical business touch. At this point, you think you can do anything! As a result, you expand your business aggressively and can even "grow yourself broke" at this stage investing too much money in expanding the company. I believe this is what we did when I was at Whittman-Hart in the early 1990s when we added too many branches around the country prematurely. Although the company had a lot of success in Chicago and Indianapolis, opening up offices in California, Virginia, and Alabama proved to be challenging. We found establishing these new offices very tough in those years despite our success in the Midwest. I made the same mistake of thinking I had the magic business touch in all three of my own businesses. In the first business, we expanded too rapidly outside of our geography. In the second and third businesses, we sold additional products we knew nothing about but thought the customer "ought to have." In all cases, it proved to be a disaster.

At this stage, Matt McCall advises, "As a rule of thumb, most firms live or die based upon their first product targeted at their core market segment. Few have the management attention span or resources to do more than this well. Furthermore, by focusing repeatedly on a given segment, you begin to gain critical mass in terms of referenceable accounts, institutional learnings, and reputation within the segment. You are also able to continually refine your product or service specifically for the needs of that market and to more effectively meet customer needs. In this business, you do not want to be a jack of all trades and master of none."

Remember the fable of the tortoise and the hare. Who won? Keep your hand on the wheel, captain. Steady as she goes.

The **T**ortoise **W**ins

_____

CELEBRATE YOUR MILESTONES

Ultimately, smaller businesses can be stronger, more flexible, and focused. With these attributes, businesses can move more quickly and respond to the immediate needs of their customers better. New ideas bubble more easily to the top. From this, these companies gain a strong advantage over their larger competitors.

Sometimes it is important to limit our ambition. I know that this sounds like heresy for the average capitalist. But constant achievement alone cannot be an end in itself. It only leads to the entrepreneur always wanting more. As business owners, we should be humble and appreciate what we have accomplished so far. There is nothing wrong with setting bold goals or searching for new opportunities in uncharted waters. This is one way that new businesses are built. But you are giving up a level of immediate satisfaction that can sustain you if you do not celebrate the milestones along the way. Once you arrive at these plateaus, ask yourself whether you can be happy if you progress no further. Yes is an acceptable answer.

Smaller and Stronger Is Good

RIGHT-SIZE YOUR DREAM

Not every business that an entrepreneur starts must have $100 million in sales and go public. These are the unrealistic dreams that were artificially pumped into the veins of start-up entrepreneurs in the 1990s. Business size is not everything. Plenty of wonderful companies never get beyond a few million dollars in sales. The owners of these businesses can live very financially successful and happy lives. Accomplishing these goals in their businesses has given them many choices.

Our dreams should be downsized to match what will make us happily successful. How do you right-size your dream? What will it take for you to feel like you have succeeded with your business? These individual benchmarks are important for you to find fulfillment in running your own business. For me, it was mostly being able to support my family and work with people I respected on my team. It was selling a customer a needed product and providing jobs to people that needed them. During the more difficult times, it was more basic like meeting payroll or paying back the money that we had borrowed from the bank. These may not sound much like dreams, but for the entrepreneur slugging it out every day in the business trenches, it's heaven.

It's OK to dream about being Bill Gates, Jeff Bezos, Jerry Yang, Mark Cuban, or Michael Dell someday. It would be fun to ring the closing bell on the New York Stock Exchange. But what happens when you realize that you don't want to be Bill or Michael? I believe that their lives are no better than yours. I'll bet that someday they even wish they were you.

F ocus on A chievable D esires

SUCCESS AS A NEAR-DEATH EXPERIENCE

Most people think that selling your business is an easy and straight-forward process. They think that selling your business happens when someone becomes interested in buying it, you negotiate a price, and then he buys your company. He then gives you a lot of money and you never see the person again. The real process is that someone gets interested, you talk about it, and then he becomes disinterested. Then you talk about it again, and you negotiate terms, and then he calls it off. He comes back again, and then you agree on a price. The buyer conducts his due diligence and finds all types of things he doesn't like so then you agree to reduce price. The most you will ever get for your business is what it says on the term sheet! You then sell your business at a lower price.

There are usually buyout incentives or warrants in which you said that this was true in your business and later on the buyer thinks that it's not true. It goes on and on and on. Selling your business is exactly the same kind of roller coaster you have been riding as you run it. Luck and timing play huge roles in selling your business.

If not for the Internet bubble, I do not imagine that my business that I sold in 1999 would be worth as much today. Just as easily, it could have gone the other way. In fact, I thought it was going the other way. I remember one day riding my bicycle to work and saying, "No, I think we are just going to close this thing up. This trip isn't worth it. I want to hit the restart button on my life. This just isn't worth it." And that day, the buyers came in with their second offer—a reconsidered offer—which was good, and then from there on, it went through. I remember sitting down and saying, "You know, I think that's it—it's over." There was more relief than chest-pounding victory.

R *est in* P *eace*

NOBODY CAN SAVE YOU—NOBODY

While running all my businesses, I always prayed at night that I would find the magic bullet that would instantly transform my company into the financial success I had hoped it would be. I looked for it in every new employee or service provider I hired. I searched for it in every call on a big prospect or every new product line I sold. Sadly, I wasted a lot of energy on my quest to find the magic bullet. I never found it.

In your business, no matter how hard you look, I'm sorry to say, you will find no savior. Many times when I become involved in a company, I can see something in the look from the business owner after our initial conversation. His face begins to brighten, and he looks at me with "savior eyes." He is looking at me as the new consultant who will "save them." This immediately worries me because I can't save them. Like me, these business owners are always looking for that magic bullet to save them from the difficult situation they live with every day. They are looking for the one thing that will finally get them over the hump, so they can relax and slow down.

Companies are built only on daily victories and learned defeats, by accomplishing small things like getting another new client or adding a great employee. Successful companies try to minimize the impact of defeats and quickly learn from them. While some companies do get that big break by attracting a large customer on which they can grow their business, don't plan on it. Even if you attain that one large customer, you still may have to deal with the additional risks of having all your "eggs in one basket." This one large customer is still no magical savior, and in the long run, brings its own set of problems and circumstances. Your one big fish in your small pond typically monopolizes all your time and has a tendency to eat any other fish swimming in the pool. This goes unnoticed until you lose this large customer and suddenly no other fish are left in your pond.

Please listen when I tell you that no one can save you. I looked everywhere so let me save you some time—stop looking. Furthermore, your search for "the one" will take up too much time and energy. It will deplete your efforts and ultimately slow the building of your business. Trust me. Only you can save yourself. Only building a solid business over time with customers who keep coming back will sustain you. Learn the patience of a business warrior who builds a company at his or her own pace, one customer at a time with no magical dust.

Business **S**aviors **A**re **E**xtinct

RUNNING ON EMPTY

You may experience hard times not because of declining sales or profit in your business. You could be making money and growing your business, but you have lost your interest. Or outside personal events are affecting your daily business life. Alternately, after five years of running your business, you realize that the company is really going nowhere or it no longer meets your career goals. You can struggle to support yourself and your other team members, but the effort hardly seems worth the results. You think that maybe it would be better to close up shop, start over, or go work for someone else. During tough economic times, this may not even be a choice for there may be no jobs available.

You are unhappy, but you are unsure of your choices. If you have a profitable business that is cash-flow positive, then you have a salable asset that someone will buy. You can seek a seller in your current business partner, other team members, channel partners, or competitors. Find someone outside your business to help you. You will not be able to rationally and emotionally negotiate the deal yourself. A friend of mine, who negotiates for a living, asks me to negotiate his personal deals for he believes that he is too close to his deals to be effective.

If your business is just making ends meet, then it may have little value to most people. Your current team members may be interested in taking it over or another company may seek value in it as a complementary revenue stream to its current business. Your business may not make sense as a stand-alone company, but may be more profitable after you are able to cut out most of the overhead and combine with another business. If you have lost your drive, look for ways to get out of your company or morph the business in another direction with the assets that you currently have. Once you have lost that passion, it is difficult to get it back unless you realize that something needs to change. You owe it to yourself and your employees to try these alternatives and not just "close up shop." In my first business, we tried to sell our company to another publishing company but we were ultimately unsuccessful. We paid back the $10,000 in loans and closed up shop. In my second business, I was kicked out of it before I had a chance to change my mind!

Something—**P**robably **Y**ou—
Needs to **C**hange

A True Tale

DAVE ORMESHER *Doing the Hokey-Pokey*

Dave Ormesher and his partner started their business, Closerlook, cold-calling from a bar. It was 1987 in Chicago, and the old Ma Bell telephone system was taking its sweet time—three weeks—to install the telephone lines for the new business.

"There's a pub just about half a block away from my office, called Brehon's Pub," Ormesher says. "We got a whole roll of quarters, and we got *Crain's* list of the top 200 companies, and we went across to the bar. There were two pay phones in the front, and we sat there and we both dialed for dollars. We just kind of went down the list and started cold-calling.

"Then we would tip the barmaid and leave the phone numbers at the pay phones as our return number, and she would answer the phone for us and take messages!" Ormesher says. "The next morning we'd come in and we'd pick up our coasters and napkins with names and phone numbers on them and we'd go back at it."

Ormesher had produced a syndicated magazine TV show called *A Closer Look*. It had been successful but still it was nearing the end of its course, and Ormesher was looking for his next gig.

"I turned to Dan Wheeler and said, 'We've made a lot of contacts out there in the business world. People really like what we do. We've got a real ability to tell a story. This seems like the ingredients for an interesting, creative marketing firm. Let's just go for it,'" Ormesher says. "So we did. We rolled the dice."

Closerlook's first client was Kraft, landed by cold-calling the receptionist and working through the telephone tree. Still, despite that initial score, Wheeler left after about a year: He didn't like not knowing whether they were going to get a paycheck from month to month.

But Ormesher kept loving it and kept going.

"In the early days, people would ask me, 'So how's it going?'" Ormesher says. "The answer was always, 'I'm having a great time,' which was code for, 'I'm not making any money yet, but I'm having a good time.'"

Ormesher says that he has always been an irrepressible optimist and that it served his business well when he was starting it up. But he doesn't confuse optimism with reckless good cheer.

"[Entrepreneurs have] really got to see the world as a place of opportunity and not as a threat," Ormesher says, "because there are going to be a lot of good days and a lot of rough days, and a lot of days—or nights, frankly, when you wake up at 3 or 4 in the morning and are staring at the ceiling, wondering how you're going to fix something.

"But when the alarm goes off at 6, you need to be the kind of person who just takes a deep breath, jumps out of bed, and is ready to take on the day again," he says.

One of Ormersher's tools is a kind of hokey-pokey—it's when you're feeling stuck, and you get out of your chair and shake things up to recharge the optimism.

"I can remember back in the early days," Ormesher says. "I'm sitting there and the clock is going, and you just wonder, what am I doing here? You have to know how to get up off your chair, throw on your coat, go for a long walk around the block a few times, get a cup of coffee, come back, and just sort of take that deep breath again, that cleansing breath, and say, 'OK, here's what we're going to do.'

"It's about getting up, out of the space that you're in, and finding another space to be at, both physically, mentally, and emotionally," Ormesher says. "Something happens and it stirs up the neurons and gets the synapses going again, and suddenly you come back with a creative insight."

Ormesher encourages his team to do the hokey-pokey whenever they feel stuck.

"Often I'll tell someone, 'It's 3 in the afternoon and you guys kind of hit a wall and you're not breaking through, get yourself up, go over to Brehon's Pub, order a pitcher, and it's amazing what happens.'"

The optimism keeps things going well especially during darker times when your team is watching for every nuance. It is manifest in what Ormesher calls the "smiling poker face."

"Optimism is so key for everyone else's emotional health," Ormesher says, "because everyone looks to you. They observe everything: They observe words. They observe actions. They observe facial expressions. I tell our management all the time, 'You've got to have a smiling poker face.'

"It's not like you're repressing your emotions or anything; it's more around self-discipline," Ormesher says. "You need to develop the self-discipline to not react, and when something is going on that you know about, you just pull it back inside and you wait until you have an opportunity to talk to an advisor or a colleague or another manager; but people really look to you for that optimistic viewpoint.

"Going through what businesses, particularly small businesses, have gone through over the past two or three years," Ormesher says, "I can tell you that I wouldn't have a company today and I wouldn't have a staff today if I did not maintain that sort of stiff upper lip and that optimistic outlook when the world was cratering around us."

Staff are whipsawed when business leaders expose them to their up-and-down emotions.

"Even in the darkest days when things don't look well and clients have fired you, and the bank's calling and vendors are calling, and people say maybe this is the end, it's like, 'No. We're going to work our way out of this. Let's just calm down. Let's look at it soberly, and let's just make a plan and make it happen. We may not turn it around in a week, but a year from now we'll be in a very different place, as long as we focus on that.'"

One of the reasons that Ormesher started Closerlook was that he wanted to build a business that fundamentally respected employees and their talents. He says that many businesses get stuck in a negative way of operating, and he has always worked to make Closerlook a positive business at its core.

"In physics, inertia is [when] an object gets to a certain speed, it tends to stay at that speed," he says. "So I think companies can have bad inertia. There's just a sense of inertia that there's really no one trying to turn the ship; it's just, that's the way it's always been, and that's the way it's always going to go. You come in, and you either adapt or you leave.

"I think there can be a positive inertia as well," he says, "where you set the ship going in the right direction, and it is self-reinforcing. . . . People suddenly recognize, wow, when I communicate, when I bring my team members in early in the process, when I trust them to do the right thing, it's reciprocated.

"In the early days when people asked, 'How's it going,' I would say, 'Well, I'm having a good time.' [I believe] you have to have that level of personal satisfaction, and you have to create an environment where you enjoy going to work every day. I'm very fortunate to be in a position to help create an environment, and in some ways create an environment that really becomes self-reinforcing; because now everybody who works here, they believe in it.

"They drink the Kool-Aid," he says. "They like coming to work, they recognize that this is kind of a special place, and they recognize how we got here. So in some ways, they're defenders of that."

One of Ormesher's main goals in starting Closerlook was to combine work with having a good time. The attitude of management seemed so counterproductive. Early in his career, when he worked for a production company, he was so frustrated by the lack of respect shown the employees that he had tried to organize a union.

"I went down to South Dearborn to the NABET office—the National Association of Broadcasting Engineers and Technicians" Ormesher says.

"And I walked in and the guy was right out of central casting with this big cigar. I said, 'We need to organize a union,' and he was like, 'All right, kid, here. Here are these cards. Take ten of them.' He said, 'If you get more than 50 percent of your workers to sign these cards, then come back to me.' So it was like the Wizard of Oz, saying, 'Bring back the broom and then we can talk [about having an election].'

"So I went back and one by one I lobbied the production team. I got them all to sign. And it was not about money, had nothing to do about money, because everybody on the team knew that we weren't rolling in the dough. We weren't necessarily asking for pay increases. It was really all about respect," Ormesher says.

"I walked back down to the NABET office with the cards in my hand and I said, 'Here we go.' He couldn't believe that I had actually pulled it off, and then he said, 'Well, you know what?' This was 1986. He goes, 'You know what? We're right in the middle of the Reagan era. This is not a great time to start a union. Unions are kind of out of favor.'

"I was totally defeated, and that was another reason why I decided to start a company, because I felt like, I think there's a better way to do this. I think if we organize a company with a culture of respect, where there's a sense of peer, colleague, respect of each other, I think we can tap into a level of creativity, energy, and productivity that will make us successful."

The culture Ormesher has created at Closerlook reflects this core value, down to the fact of its open office plan.

"There are no cubicles or no private offices. I don't have a private office, I don't have a cube. My desk is in a corner out with probably eight other people, and it sends a strong message that we're all in this together," he says. "It's not even an open-door policy; it's a no-door policy. You need to talk, you need to grab a cup of coffee, let's go."

Ormesher says that staffing is the most important strategic process for a start-up.

"Your brand, your success, and how much you even enjoy your job is directly related to your ability to hire," Ormesher says. "When I first started hiring staff, back when we were maybe three or four people, it just occurred to me that, jeez, we hired this person; they're now 25 percent of the presence of our firm. We'd better get this right."

Over the years, Ormesher's firm has evolved a three-stage hiring process that grew out of Ormesher's recognition of his own blind spots. The first interview is pretty informal and is conducted by the executive sponsoring the hire.

The firm's philosophy is to always hire people smarter than you are, so that you can raise the average IQ of the firm rather than lower it. If the candidate passes, they move on to stage two, where they are grilled by a group of people from the competency area they would be working in.

"It's definitely grueling, and it's at every level," Ormesher says. "So if they're coming in to do sales, then they meet up with all the other account people, salespeople. If they're a designer, they bring in their portfolio and they really go through it with all the designers."

The final interview is the decisive test. It's called the "gauntlet," and Ormesher seldom attends.

"The candidate is ushered into the conference room, where there are 12 people around the table," he says. "They're from every functional competency area within the company, and they spend about an hour. This is really a culture fit interview. As light as we try to make it, it is really intimidating when they walk in and see all these people who, most of them, they don't know.

"This is really about attitude," Ormesher says. "It's about humility. It's about their ability to express themselves. Because we believe very strongly that everyone in the organization needs to be able to have client face time. It's also a very interesting test of what happens when you're thrown in front of a room of 12 people and you're asked questions that you had not expected, out of left field. How do you respond? Do you freeze? Do you clam up? Do you get hostile?

"To this day, when people go out for a drink, they'll get on the subject of, what was your gauntlet like," Ormesher says. "People remember the questions they were asked; they remember who was in the room. They tease each other for asking them bizarre questions, and it's part of the process of getting inculcated to the culture.

"When the gauntlet is over and the candidate is escorted out—'We'll be in touch, we'll give you a call tomorrow'—we come back together and there's a full debrief. If it's thumbs-down, the candidate doesn't get hired. We really try to go for consensus.

"Because of that process, there are a lot of people now who are invested in that person's success, because no one wants to feel like, "Oh, jeez, I was in the gauntlet and I missed that, and we had to fire that person." There are a lot of people who are invested in the new candidate's success in the company.

"There was a very senior-level executive within the pharmaceutical industry on the East Coast that I was very keen on hiring. I flew him out to Chicago and we met; we went out to dinner. I was like, 'This guy is golden. He's just going to totally supercharge our business.' And someone reminded me, 'Well, don't you think some other folks should talk to him?' I said, 'Oh, OK, fine, whatever. We'll just go through the process.'

"So we brought him back in, and he interviewed with about eight other senior people and salespeople, and just more kind of an informal gauntlet. I was not present in the meeting. So he came out, we shook hands, and I said, 'Listen, this is great. Thanks for coming to Chicago. We'll be in touch here in the next day to start talking about your comp package and negotiation and everything.' And he said, 'OK, great.' So he left for the airport.

"I walked back into the conference room and I almost had a mutiny on my hands. They were like, 'No way.' I said, 'What are you talking about? Look at his credentials. I've really gotten to know him.' They said, 'Well, maybe you got to know him, and maybe he was respectful when you were in the room, but he was a total jackass with us. He was arrogant. He just kind of saw us as, this is a perfunctory exercise, and I'm really going to report to Dave, so I don't know why I'm even talking to you.' There was another side to him that came out.

"It was devastating to me, for a couple of reasons: One, I couldn't believe I didn't see it, so that was a—talk about humility; it was like, OK, well, there's my blind spot. Second, obviously I really need this other perspective. There was no way I could hire him. And I had to call him up the next day and say, 'You flunked the gauntlet, buddy, and this is why.'

"That solidified in everyone's minds that we need to abide by this process, and whenever we try to short-circuit the process, we regret it later."

8

FINDING CUSTOMERS
Not a Small Detail

SHOW ME YOUR CUSTOMERS

I remember the famous refrain from Tom Cruise's movie *Jerry Maguire* where Rod Tidwell, a football player, keeps saying to his agent, "Show me the money!" The mantra for any entrepreneur building a business should be, "Show me the customers!" So many entrepreneurs talk about the business they are building. But you don't have a "business" until you have customers. Until someone actually pays you money to do something for them, and you collect that money, you do not have a business no matter how many people you employ or how great the office is that you rent.

I remember telling my partner in my last business that I loved our company, except for the fact that I had to deal with customers and vendors. Without them, no one would be making our business confusing or taking us off track. Of course, without vendors and customers we would not have had a business, but I figured that was a small detail. Customers will wreak havoc on the pristine business plan and vision you have developed for your company. If you are economically able to have a "business" without customers, then I applaud you. No one will come to your door and make you uncomfortable. No one will question your assumptions or ask you to rethink your business model. Congratulations! Come to the office every day and enjoy your hobby. This part of your life will be conflict-free. It will also be challenge-free. Read no further in this book. Please pass it to someone who actually has to build a real business.

Now, for the rest of us, those of us who need to make money while we pursue our passions and interests, customers make a business real. Look no further. Customers are the only real secret sauce there is. If you have paying customers, you have the business world by the string. You have choices. Customers will daily test your assumptions and actions against the market.

Without Customers, You Have a Hobby

OUTLAW PREMEDITATED ENTREPRENEURIAL BUSINESS

I think in the 1990s so many people thought too much about starting businesses. As discussed before, their goal was to start a business that would make them money. While you can't go to jail for it yet, I think that "premeditated business" should be against the entrepreneurial law. This happens in two ways. If you think too much about your business, how you will structure it and what you will sell, you may never get started. You will spend far too much time and money thinking about starting a business rather then actually starting one. Your business only really starts when you begin talking to customers and asking them if they want to buy something. Before you sell that first product or service to a customer and they pay you for it, no matter what name you give to it, you are not running a business. You are working at a hobby that is being subsidized by your savings or friends and family.

Primarily, I tell entrepreneurs to think for a short period of time, make a decision, and then do. The market will teach you more than you can ever learn from planning.

For example, I know Seth, who was a very successful engineer for many years. He left his job and wanted to start an online business that distributed all types of motors. He was passionate that this was what the industry needed. He spent hundreds of thousands of dollars of his own money getting ready to start his business. He spent money writing a business plan with consultants. He spent money developing a sophisticated Web site to run his business even though he had no customers. He spent money advertising his business but had no way to follow up with the few customers that called. After a year of planning and spending all this money, a few customers did start to come after an aggressive online campaign. At this point, when Seth realized that the business was actually talking to customers and trying to sell them motors, he lost interest in the business. He has more interest in "starting" a business than running or building one.

Similarly, Joan loved everything Greek. She wanted to start a Web site in the major cities in the United States that would feature Greek objects for people to buy. She envisioned expanding to every major city. She surveyed potential providers and customers on her idea. Joan said they were excited about it but during this entire process she never asked either the provider or the customer whether they wanted to spend money with her and advertise on her Web site. She was afraid that they would say no and didn't want any bad feedback to "impair" her vision of this business. Until Joan actually asks a customer for money for a service or product she can buy, she has no business, just a hobby. A vision untested against market reality is just philosophical fantasy. It makes paying business bills tough.

Start by Asking a Customer

EVERYONE IS A SUSPECT, BUT EVERYONE IS NOT A CUSTOMER

Everyone is not a customer. One solution does not fit all. Your customers are only those prospects for whom you can profitably solve a problem. But as discussed earlier, through networking, every contact may lead you to a significant customer. Still everyone that fits your prospect profile may not be a good customer. Prospects must want to buy something fairly close to what you are selling, so you can collect their money and make a profit at it. In fact, a customer who does not pay or is always unhappy with your service is not a benefit to you. His status as an ex-customer may help you more. Send him to your competition. This may be a real boost to your business!

Prospects may also want to buy something that you do not sell. In this case, you are confronted with the difficult task of simultaneously balancing your need to be focused with your need to be flexible. The solution is to sell to the prospect what is in your product line or service arsenal. Today, this is how you will make money. At the same time, listen to the prospects and hear what they need so you can evolve your business in the direction of the market. You can't be everything to everybody. But you can steer your business 25 degrees in either direction to grow. This decision on whether to go where your prospect wants you to go is tricky. A large amount of analysis will get you nowhere. If you choose wrong and this new area distracts you too much or proves not to be profitable (because you have never done this before), it is another potential minefield for your company.

Make the decision by answering a few questions. Ask yourself how much you need the money from this new source of business. How successful are sales of your main products? If your main business is strong, and you do not need the cash, pass on this new opportunity. Or test it on a limited basis, which would not hurt your company. This is the best-case scenario, so you have a choice. If your main business is weak, and you need the money, you have no choice but to see whether this new opportunity can generate cash.

Be **F**ocused and **F**lexible **T**hen **D**ecide

DESPERATION HAS AN ODOR

Your quest for paying customers is central to your daily business life. Everything else is a distant second. This message was lost to many who started businesses during the Internet bubble. I know for I was there, and I did it, too.

The quest for customers should be done in a level-headed and consistent manner. It can't be frantic, rushed, or hopeless. The paradox is that these feelings might arise, especially because you probably really want paying customers so you can keep your business going. No matter how bad things get, when searching for customers don't panic. Prospective customers can feel desperate companies, and this will hurt your chances of landing the sale. Few people want to do business with someone who desperately needs it to keep his or her business's doors open. Your attitude will transmit this in all your interactions, and it will lead to them not buying your product or services. This is one of the very tricky parts about growing your business. How can you exude confidence about your products or services when you need customers so badly? Practice your pitch, and maybe even take acting lessons. Try to never be in the place where landing one customer will make or break your company. Breathe. Learn to check your anxiety at the door at least for the length of a sales call.

Customers Buy Confidence

HOW MUCH IS THAT PUPPY IN THE WINDOW?

For a business starting out, pricing what you sell sometimes is very easy. Look at what the competition is doing, and price your products higher or lower depending on your desired positioning in the marketplace. Test the supply-and-demand curve to see how you can maximize your price and the quantity you want to be sold. Evaluate what people pay now to solve their problem and price your product at a better value. Sometimes, pricing what you sell is difficult because it is a service or other intangible product that is closely tied to who you are. This may actually feel like you are pricing or selling yourself for you are the leader of the business!

Many people are more comfortable exchanging services than selling their services outright, because in this case everyone gets something out of it, and everyone wins without having to talk about cash. But when you sell your services for money, everyone still wins. The customer gets your excellent service, and you get money to buy other services or pay your employees.

Remember, prospects reject sales proposals for all types of reasons. Many of these have nothing to do with you but rather with internal company politics, past relationships, or timing issues. Two different companies with the same problem may come to totally different decisions about your product. You need to find the one that wants to buy your solution.

It is also a difficult transition for many entrepreneurs to go from surveying customers about interest in their product to asking them to buy it. If simply asked for their opinion, most prospects will be kind to you and give you a positive answer. Few people like conflict, so these people support you and give you the answer that you want. For example, one business I invested in had 75,000 visitors to its Web site every month. When we surveyed a sample of them to see if they would pay $5 a month to visit the site, 95 percent said yes. When the company implemented this subscription model, less than 5,000 of the visitors agreed to pay. This is why it is a lot easier to run a business as a hobby where you do not need financial gain. In this case, you never have to ask anyone for money or try to achieve any results from the market!

Asking someone for money is one of the most difficult things we can do in the business world. None of us likes rejection. It always feels so personal. But the yes or no by the customer on whether they want to buy your product is an immediate vote on what your company is doing. Prospects don't vote with words, they vote with their checkbooks. You need these affirmations or rejections so you can figure out which direction is best for growing your company. This type of feedback is the only kind that counts. It immediately makes your business real. Whether you enjoy it or not, this is what you want and need to evolve. Your goal for any prospect should be to get a decision, any decision. So many company proposals seem to end with no decision at all.

But if a prospect does not get back to you in a timely manner on your proposal, you have your answer. Realize that it's a no. Take her off your prospect list no matter how promising she is. Stop going down that mouse hole chasing this cheese. Seek buyers elsewhere. Your energy will be a lot more productive searching in a new place for a prospect who actually wants to buy from you.

I*f* I*t* B*ites*, Y*ou* D*on't* W*ant* I*t*

DO BUSINESS WITH PEOPLE WHO WANT TO DO BUSINESS WITH YOU

I have always strove to do business with people and companies that want to do business with me. Trying to get a prospect to do business with you when she really is not interested is a losing proposition. On paper, your product may be a terrific solution for her company, but in reality, she does not want to buy it. You may never know why. Acknowledge the fact that it is time to move on to someone who actually wants to do business with you. This simple bond of forming a relationship where two companies want to do business with each other is critical. The way that a lot of business is conducted is by two people from two companies who want to be in business with each other. As the old adage says, "People do business with people they like." Many times, in this relationship of "the willing," they find a way to work together. This is another aspect where business again is really only about people. Additionally, the acquisition costs of landing this type of customer is a lot less and the opportunity to continue to do more business with them in the future on a repeated basis is greatly increased.

This is where building relationships with people and waiting for timing and luck once again come into the picture. If you form good business relationships with prospective clients, you have positioned yourself for luck and timing to swing your way. A prospect who wants to do business with you will eventually find a way to do it. One day he simply picks up the phone to call you when he has a problem your company can solve.

Position Yourself through Relationships

"It's always the catch-22. 'Well, you have no experience in our business.' 'Well, the only way I can get experience is if you hire me.' It's a catch-22, and that's why relationship selling—consultative selling, but relationship selling—is so important at the beginning. It's all about networking. You almost de facto come to it from a sense of humility, because there's not a lot you can talk about."

Dave Ormesher

EVERYONE SELLS

This is not the 1990s. Rest in peace. As an entrepreneur you will have to actually go out and sell things to prospective customers no matter who else is involved in your business. This is one mission that at some level you are unable to delegate at the beginning. If you do not like to sell, do not start your own business. This is yet another reason to get a job that you are comfortable with.

In a small business, one thing can be counted on: Everyone sells. Only sales will build your business, nothing else. Forget all the fancy marketing positioning of your company, or the design of great logos and stationery. Selling to customers is the key. Think of your business as you in a lifeboat on a rough sea. Your only choice is for everyone to row.

If you are afraid to sell, you have two choices: You can get over it or get a job. Actually, your only other choice is to find a partner who wants to do the selling while you do the development or operations part of the business. While you may not be selling to external product customers, you will still need to sell your ideas to your team and vendors. But be warned that this will give a tremendous amount of leverage to your partner in controlling the business. Your partner will in be a stronger position because he or she, not you, will have relationships with your customers. Ultimately, there is no escape except to develop some skills of your own in this area.

You can try to take a selling class if it helps you learn these skills. But keep your expectations low, since typically it is not easy to apply techniques that you have learned in a "live" situation. With the help of your partner or mentor, find a new prospect and go along on the sales call. Listen and learn until it's your turn next time. When you fail, ask the prospect why he or she did not buy your product and move on to the next one. The best door-to-door salespeople of the last century used this tried-and-true method of improving their sales skills. When one door closed in their faces, they went next door and knocked on that one. It certainly gives you the practice that you need.

Another important aspect of selling is to carefully ensure that each team member is contributing to the bottom line of the company on a daily basis. Every employee should ask himself or herself this question every day: "Did I make money for the company today?" In any entrepreneurial venture, there is simply no room to put people in the "overhead" category. You are unable to have anyone on the team who is not vital to obtaining, or retaining, customers.

Start-Ups Have No Overhead

"I hate getting calls from salespeople who want to sell me something and they're reading the script. They don't understand the product or the service or really what the solution is."

"When you embody the solutions, like I know the solution inside and out, and you're passionate about it, that makes all the difference in the world."

Stephanie Covall-Pinnix

FIND YOUR MOTIVATION

We each will find our primary motivation for selling in different places. I hate cold calling. I knew that when I started all my businesses. But I also knew that if I didn't cold-call, then I wouldn't sell anything, and I wouldn't be able to feed my family. I had to discipline myself to face this fear every single day. I remember days sitting alone in my small office staring at the computer screen with the list of people I "wanted" to call that day, and finding any reason to get up from my desk so I would not have to call. Finally, I would get up the courage to call, half hoping to encounter voice mail.

For me, this fear was based on a fear of personal rejection. It did not make logical sense for most of the people that I called did not know me, and I had never met them. But somehow, because I was the designated sales leader for my start-up, my success or failure on the phone became a measure of who I was as a person. For some strange reason, I sometimes changed my voice on the phone to a different accent when I made cold calls. I guess this was an additional layer of protection for myself. Just remember, prospects on the phone can't bite. Even if they could, call my friend Zane and he'll tell you that "the worst they can do is eat you, and that's illegal."

As long as sales were my primary responsibility, and cold calling was our main method of acquiring customers, it never got easier for me. Not even a bit. But I did it and many times did it well.

If this is difficult for you, find a way to locate your motivation. Pictures of your family in your office might help. Breaking your calling goals down into smaller chunks may help as well. If you call enough people, you will find prospects who are interested in what you have to sell. Your job is to make prospects aware of what you offer so when they are ready to buy, they think of your company. Stop thinking about it as selling, and start thinking of it as more like telling them what is for sale. Tell them you will be there when they are ready to buy.

And **U**se **I**t

DEMAND AND SUPPLY

Does lowering your price increase your sales? There is that economic principle that we learned in school that demand goes up if the price is lower. This does not really work in starting or running a small business. In this case, market demand, or, more simply, what your prospects want to buy, is tied to the value they alone place on your products, and the alternatives they have to solve the problem you are trying to sell them. Most times, entrepreneurs set the price of the products too low in the marketplace because they think they can only compete based on price. This backfires on them as prospects see little value in these low-priced products or services and do not buy them. Carefully look to see what prospects pay to solve the problem your solution addresses and price your products accordingly. Remember, it is easier to lower your price then to raise it.

You can also test various prices in the market to see if your sales increase or decrease by lowering or raising your prices. You may be surprised by how little your price on this microeconomic level actually affects demand. I know at least one business that prices its product up or down solely based on the customer's budget for their solution.

You **H**ave **M**ore **P**ower
Than **Y**ou **T**hink

A True Tale

MOHNISH PABRAI

Heads You Win, Tails You Don't Lose Much

Mohnish Pabrai was born and raised in India and is the son of an entrepreneur. His father was bankrupt on many an occasion and started (and sometimes failed) businesses. As a result, Pabrai doesn't have much in the way of financial fear.

"When I can to the United States, I was very used to a feast or famine kind of lifestyle," Pabrai says. "For me, I view all my businesses as games. It is almost like a game of Monopoly. I think of them as exciting Monopoly games.

"There is this notion that entrepreneurs are risk takers," he says. "I think this notion is wrong. When I started my business, I viewed staying in Tellabs doing what I was doing as a very high-risk situation. I thought, if I can go set up a company and it does OK, then that is more interesting.

"Basically what entrepreneurs do is they are arbitrage players," he says. "They look at the landscape and they find a gap, something that they believe is a product or service that they could offer that the world wants. And they go do it.

"I was looking at the technology space. We found the gap." He says. "We had this very focused set of offerings. [At the time] customers who wanted those kinds of solution had no choice but to go to a start-up.

"Heads I win, and tails I don't lose much," he says. "In effect, the downside was nonexistent. And the upside was significant."

Pabrai was working at Tellabs when he went for it and started his first company, TransTech, 13 years ago. Pabrai capitalized it using $30,000 from his 401(k) and an additional $70,000 from credit cards.

Pabrai was 24 years old and single. He figured the worse that could happen would be bankruptcy.

"I researched personal bankruptcy law," he says, "and I found that basically if you can't cover all your debts, you declare personal bankruptcy. It will clear you out, and you get a fresh, clean start.

"I had nothing to lose," he says. "Let's say the company didn't work. Then I declare personal bankruptcy. The credit-card companies don't get paid unfortunately. And I get back on track. There are not a lot of bad things that can happen to you. Personal bankruptcy actually improves your credit."

"Plus, my employer told me that I could come back at any time," he says. "So I knew I could go have fun for a year."

Pabrai was working full-time at Tellabs, and part-time on his business, while he collected every credit card he could find.

"As soon as I had some revenue from the business," he says, "I quit my job. I charged back and forth between the credit cards. In the meantime, the business was growing. In 1991, I did about half a million in revenue. It was growing very fast, faster than the cash I could generate."

"I borrowed from Peter to pay Paul," he says. "As soon as one credit card would fill up, I would use the next one.

"I had payroll coming up," he says, "and I had no money for payroll. Then I hit the limit on all the credit cards, the money was all gone. I went to friends of mine, who took $25,000 out on their credit cards to lend to me.

"My business was growing faster than the cash was coming in," he says. "I could see around the corner that cash would catch up. I would go to all these banks [for a loan] and they would say you must be crazy."

Finally, one banker understood the business, and set Pabrai up with a line of credit and helped him clean up the credit-card debt.

"I got set up properly with a banking relationship," he says. "Eventually, the business was doing $20 million in sales and we had a $3 million credit line from the same banker. It was a huge adrenalin rush. It was fun.

"The turning point for the company came in March 1991 when I went to meet the CIO of Case Corporation," Pabrai says. "I had never met this person or had any interaction with him before. I spoke to him for two minutes on the phone. I went in to see him, where he basically spent about three minutes asking me about what I did.

"Then he wrote me a note," Pabrai says. "And he said there is a man outside my office who is my purchasing officer. We want your team on-site in four weeks. He gave us a purchase order for half a million dollars as a starter right there.

"What I discovered is that he had a pain point," Pabrai says "And what we offered was right on to take care of that pain point.

"I was so elated because at that point I knew that the company would not go under," Pabrai says. "I knew with absolute certainty that we would not go out of business. There was very clear certainty.

"I still remember that rush," Pabrai says. "The rush I felt on that drive back from Racine has never since been replicated because it was so amazing. I was so elated with this 15-minute sales call with someone I didn't know giving me this big chunk of business.

"I saw this two- to three-year window where someone could step in and clean up. And that is what we did," he says. "Every two to three years we had to redo the business. We actually jumped through two to three curves in ten years, it had shifted so much.

"Now those guys who lent me the $25,000 say they wished they had asked for equity," he says. They were good buddies, and they still are.

9

BACK TO THE PAST

"Retropreneurs" from the
Merchant Class

A NEW GENERATION OF ENTREPRENEURS

Business prosperity from March 1991 to March 2001 was one of the longest on record according to the National Bureau of Economic Research. As a result of this extended time of prosperity, we have forgotten a lot of basic business skills. We need to create a new generation of entrepreneurs for this decade. The business cycle has evolved once again, and the paradigm has shifted backward.

The Internet boom was characterized by executives who were paid a lot of money, and stock options that shifted the focus of these companies away from customers or revenue and toward the financial aspect of driving up the stock price. We were building stock value but not sustainable business value. As we have seen, stock prices go up and down every day. Business value evolves much more slowly over a long period of time. It seems silly to think now how many Internet start-ups had stock values greater than General Motors in 1999.

The characteristics of the new generation of entrepreneurs for the 2000s look a lot like the characteristics of businesspeople from 200 years ago. They are people starting businesses because they had no choice and because they need a way to support their families. They are also people driven by passion. They use their own savings, and that of their families to get started. They realize that being an entrepreneur is a lifestyle not an exit strategy. They know they need to be patient and stay with it for ten years. Finally, they know that this is the way businesses have been built for all of time. They know they are not alone.

The realism that starting a business is hard is again taking hold. Hard is OK because that is the way it was meant to be. People were meant to build their companies slowly, one customer at a time. Like merchants, we are selling things to each other again, not to the analysts that will hype the financial value of our company.

If this is the way it is now, will we lose the innovation that was so incredibly rich in the 1990s? I don't think so. Despite all the money that the capital markets pumped into new business ideas, I question how many true innovations were made. Certainly, selling dog food on the Internet was innovative but not a profitable business model. The only truly innovative model that is purely Internet would be eBay, which was launched in 1995. It is a global trading platform where tens of millions of users can buy and sell goods and services. According to eBay's Web site, people spend more time on eBay than on any other online site. In 2002, eBay members bought and sold about $15 billion in goods and services.

Often true innovation comes from funded research. But a lot of innovation comes from people accidentally discovering things when they are trying to solve a practical problem. For example, 3M Post-it notes were only started because a friend used the inventor's "weak glue" to stick markers into his hymnal for his music. When Procter & Gamble came out with Pampers, they were marketed as portable diapers to use when you traveled with your baby. They never thought it would replace cloth diapers permanently.

They're Retropreneurs

REEMERGENCE OF THE MERCHANT CLASS

We have gone back to our business past. In the 2000s, as it has been for centuries, business has returned to being about people—people buying and selling things or services to each other because there is a need and an offer to fill that need. It may not exactly be the old-time market place with merchants lining up on either side in rows, but it's close. We are aided in selling things to each other with some new communication technologies but not all of them are helpful. Things like video teleconferencing and video phones haven't really been integrated into mainstream American business. The technology is there, but people still want to do business with other people they can see and hear in person. In some way they need to form that trust with them.

With lower demand during hard times, sellers need to go out and seek buyers. Like the merchants in our past, they will find these buyers from the people they meet who recommend them to other people. Although this is the Information Age, we are going back to the reemergence of the merchant class. The merchant class of the Middle Ages drove commerce. They used their skilled hands to provide a service or product usually from their own businesses. They were tradesman and storeowners in a marketplace. We're not all standing in a marketplace anymore where people are coming and showing their wares. But we almost have this on the Internet where anyone can go and "browse" your products as though they were in an open marketplace. Unfortunately, what we found out in the 1990s is that having a fancy Web site to show your products doesn't drive sales. Marketing may attract customers, but people forming relationships sell products. We are using new forms of communication to form relationships through e-mail, instant messaging, and cell phones. But the basis for these relationships remain the same. You have something I need to buy and I trust you enough to buy it from you. Despite all the efficient electronic communication tools, the entrepreneur still needs to see herself as a merchant—someone going out into the world proactively and selling her products "on the street" in front of people.

During hard economic times, there's a lot more bartering going on like in the Middle Ages. People may not have money during difficult times, but they do have skills they can trade with others. This has worked particularly well for me. I have bartered my business skills for everything from family cooking lessons to computer equipment to massage therapy services.

The reemergence of the merchant class can drive the American economy out of any challenging economic times. We will do this one sale at a time.

Recovery **W**ill **C**ome **O**ne **S**ale at a **T**ime

LOSING GROUND, LOST GROUND

Former U.S. President Harry Truman best described how most people define bad times. He said that "it's a recession when your neighbor loses his job; it's a depression when you lose yours." I define bad times as when your pay gets cut at your current job. It's when you are fired and you can't find work for many months. It's when the value of your savings or investments keeps shrinking annually rather than growing as you expected. It's that feeling of losing ground every year rather than saving for the future. But now during these days of difficult economic decline, I can barely peek at the reports that come from my money managers even on a quarterly basis. I do not think I can add to the daily economic burden of knowing how much more money I lost.

Few jobs and a sinking stock market put a general malaise of gloom and doom on the market. The news media dutifully broadcasts all these layoffs and losses every day. Because businesses are made up of people, this overall personal discomfort we all have gradually spreads to every person's business decision making in the economy. The result is that over time, decision makers get scared and become very conservative. They try not to hire new employees. They begin to pull back on their purchasing decisions. They stop buying things from other companies that they do not absolutely need today. They stop making investments in the future of their companies. In turn, businesses that were selling them products and services begin to lose money and let their employees go. As the company is losing money, it stops making new purchases and investments. This cycle goes on like this throughout the economy. This spiraling effect means that tough business times are here.

But hard times can be good times too. It is a great time for people to pull together and help each other instead of pounding their chests and saying how successful they are. During prosperous times, everybody is a winner and they want to stop and tell you about it. As the old mariner's philosophy says, "The incoming tide rises all boats." We were all brilliant businesspeople in 1999. But there was also no panacea during these times of prosperity. As the stories filtered through the news of how seemingly everyone was striking it rich, many people had that nagging feeling that they were falling behind. They were not making "as much" money as their neighbor and had to keep up with the "Joneses." Unfortunately, people still find ways to torture themselves during the good times too.

Hard Times Are Good Times Too

"In a terrible market, you have to have really good management. You have to be able to look at the business and see the really hard things you need to do. You have to find a way to keep your people engaged and motivated even though they are involved in something that is less pleasant."

John Banta

GOOD TIMES CAN BREED WASTE

During the 1990s, there was a general feeling of euphoria every day as we knew we were all geniuses in the stock market. Even if we had had a rough day at work, we could go home and look at the big rise in the stock market, and feel that we had made a dollar that day. Regardless of what happened at work, we felt financially secure. During these times, I remember downloading the value of my stock portfolio into QuickBooks to greedily see what I had made that day. Selfishly, it made me feel good and secure.

All this chest pounding not only wastes money but also diverts the entrepreneur from focusing on business. As I have mentioned, great times make the business owner feel that he or she can do everything. You'll feel like you can do everything and even brag to others about your brilliant success. This happened during 1990 at Whittman-Hart. We had been so successful selling consulting services in the Midwest, that we decided to "build on our success" and open up fancy offices in the West and Southeast. More press releases and chest pounding followed. These offices did not succeed and ended up costing the company a lot of money. We did not realize the challenges of selling services in other markets where the company brand was not known and where the geography made it difficult for our consultants to travel for sales activities.

I made a similar mistake when in my last company we decided to help a friend of mine start a company at our office that had nothing to do with our business. We thought we had plenty of energy and could do anything. In the long run, it hurt our business and my friend's business because of the lack of support we could give him.

Forget the **C**hest **P**ounding

DIG DEEPER FOR PROFIT

When times get rough, you are not alone. Typically, a bad economy affects everyone. The good news about this is that hard times do breed the essential business skill of humility. When you know that you can fail, it makes you respect the hard-fought success that you and others have had even more. During difficult times, cooperation becomes economically advantageous again for there are not enough resources or profit margins for any one business to do it on its own. We all need to help each other. Working diligently with other businesses through hard times actually binds people together. It may only start from the basic need of "I scratch your back, and you scratch mine." Even if it begins out of this selfish instinct, people wanting to help you to get something in return at least starts the process moving in the right direction. In the end, accomplishing something as a team is one of the most satisfying outcomes any businessperson can achieve.

A $50 million company I know had been in business for almost 100 years. Historically, it is only able to deliver 5 percent net profit to the bottom line. Sales have grown slowly over the years, so there was never a need to make any changes because it could predict what it could contribute to the parent company. A few years back, poor sales hit its industry particularly hard. No matter how the company calculated it, a 50 percent drop in sales was going to mean disaster for its overall profit contribution. The CEO needed to find ways to cut the company's expenses or increase its gross profit while not cutting revenue. The company was able to do this by throwing out established distribution channel assumptions, cutting discounts for many vendors, and raising prices for newer products to its customers. It would not have even thought of doing this unless it had hit bad economic times and sales had shrunk. As a result, the company was able to deliver the same dollar profit to the parent corporation. Now that times are better, and sales have grown again, it is able to keep the same percent net income and actually raise its contribution to the parent company. Without these bad times, the CEO would never have questioned his assumptions and never been able to raise his percentage of contribution. Tough times forced him to dig deeper, challenge decade-old assumptions, and find profit that he and the company are now able to take advantage of during the good times!

You'll Emerge Stronger

IF YOU PROSPER, WHILE OTHERS CRASH

Your business may be countercyclical to the general market economy. While others are crashing, you may be prospering. What do you do if other businesses are having a tough time and your business is growing and profitable? First, be thankful. Next, don't brag. Be humble because your turn will probably come someday. You won't want others to throw it in your face when your time comes. Use your time to buy and leverage cheap resources. This may be in terms of people, product lines, or new investments. Use your financial strength to expand into areas where your weaker competitors are. Balance caution with the opportunistic time to expand. At the same time, go out of your way to help your employees, vendors, or others associated with your business if they are in need. All these people will remember your actions during their time of need and you will build plenty of relationship capital.

Save for a rainy day. Very few businesses are recession-proof. You can be sure that the business cycle will move and you will find yourself during those times on the losing side of the economy.

P*itch* **I***n,* **H***elp, and* **S***ave for* **Y***our* **R***ainy* **D***ay*

DEFINING SUCCESS

I have come to think that my definition of financial success is to have enough money so I can afford to have someone clean my bathroom. Bob Okabe points out that in some countries, just having a bathroom is a sign of success!

I met with a banker the other day to discuss the future of one of the companies of which I am chairman of the board. He asked me what the company's goal was for this year. I said, "To survive." He seemed to accept this answer well. Another growing sign of how far we are getting from the Internet bubble days.

Some of our psychic energy has been sapped by the fact that Generation X and Y businesspeople (those born after 1965) might not be financially better off than our parents. This does not fit the past 100 years of the American dream that says every generation becomes more financially successful. Our parents taught us that if we go to a good college and work hard, we will have a bigger house than they do. This was easy to say because, many times, their families were immigrants. They were sometimes the first of their generation to go to college. This has changed with our generation. It is difficult for us to accept for our parents have the same hopes and dreams for us that their parents had for them.

D*efine* **S***uccess for* **Y***ourself*

TIME HEALS ALL WOUNDS

We are all mourning the 1990s and the bursting of the Internet bubble. In the early 2000s, we are not in a place too dissimilar from where we were during the recessionary times of the 1980s and 1990s. It only seems worse because we can still remember the best times that U.S. business has had in the past 50 years. Once we have forgotten about this Internet blip on our radar screen and are able to distance ourselves from the 1990s, we will actually feel like we are in a better place. We will realize that it was just an economic anomaly and there weren't that many sustained economic gains. If you truly look around, a lot of people road the wave up and almost as many people road it down. As these stories are now getting told and we get farther from the 1990s, all types of people who supposedly made money really did not. This may make some of us feel better that we were not left out.

Stop mourning. The more quickly we forget about the 1990s bubble, the better. It was just a mirage. Accept that it is never coming back. Return to the business basics that have worked for thousands of years: Passion. Customers. Cash flow.

Forget the 1990s

A True Tale
PENNY PICKETT
Polishing the Diamonds in the Rubble

Penny Picket started her calligraphy business in 1980. At the time, she had no idea that it would become a technology company. But her business, like so many businesses fueled by passion do, morphed way beyond her initial imaginings into the unexpected.

"We started out as a service business doing calligraphy and graphic design, which was fairly typical for a woman in 1980," she says. "From there, we fell into doing some work with software engineers on translating fonts, colors, design elements into a programmable language for PCs that were really starting to come online in the early 1980s.

"When I started [my business, people would respond with] a pat on the head, particularly when I still had things in the house. 'Oh, isn't that sweet? She's doing a little home-based business.'"

But Pickett says she saw that attitude toward her business and other start-ups change soon after as businesses built around the culture of *The Organization Man* thinned their ranks. This was the seminal book that discussed 20-, 30-, and 40-year careers with one corporation.

"I was relieved after the layoffs in the 1980s—and a lot of the men started [businesses]. I started hearing the word *entrepreneur* for the first time. It had a lot to do with the social context in which this was happening."

Pickett sees a possible parallel between business start-up trends and innovation during the 1980s and today. Our current downturn could incubate future waves of innovation.

"Early in the 1980s, a lot of people were getting pink slips. A lot of them, out of desperation, turned to their garage or their basements and said, 'Now what am I going to do?' This is a question I think about with this downturn and a lot of people getting pink slips; does this mean that we're going to get another wave of new businesses?'

A basic tenet of *The Organization Man* was the idea that an employee gave the corporation loyalty and, in turn, the corporation took care of you. Those days are long gone, and with their demise, many of us have adopted business behaviors formerly exclusive to entrepreneurs, Pickett says.

"Because of what's going on around them, people today are much more flexible and much more entrepreneurial, even if they do go to big companies. They're always realizing that there may be a time for them to go off and start a business," she says.

"I think more people are biting the bullet and learning a lot of the characteristics of entrepreneurs," she says. But "deep down inside, if they had a choice, they probably would like a less stressed and more comfortable life."

An important legacy of the 1990s might be a more accepting culture of entrepreneurship with a newly established federal system of support that will bolster the next generation of entrepreneurs, Pickett says. We might also see more entrepreneurs 35 years of age and older.

"Los Alamos will now allow their scientists to go on entrepreneurial leave, if they want to take their ideas out of the lab," she says. "They're trying to help them minimize that risk, so they will give them the three years to go off and try starting a company.

"Now the scientists know that if it doesn't work, they have the security of coming back in and doing additional research. The fact that the federal government is encouraging this behavior is such a phenomenal difference," she says.

"Even as everything crashes, we're still ahead of where it was before," she says. "The next push starts at a higher level. It's fascinating to watch the transition. The rock is a whole lot further up the hill."

A True Tale
TROY HENIKOFF
Spinning Gold from Bubblegum and Duct Tape

Troy Henikoff is back to tinkering in his basement again. He won't say with what. The shadows are getting longer. The dark side is advancing.

"I've got folding tables and chairs set up down there," Henikoff says. "A couple of weeks ago, my wife looked at me and asked, 'Is this going to be like SurePayroll again?'

"We got married four weeks after I founded SurePayroll," he says. "We bought a house four months later, and had the baby ten months after that. My wife was miserable . . . she felt like she was doing it alone."

He's transitioning out of SurePayroll now. Recently, he took his wife and daughter traveling on a sabbatical for six months. He's spent the first months of 2003 figuring out what's next. "I like to create something from nothing," he says. "Sculpting from a vacuum.

"You need enough activity around you where you start to feel the intensity and the progress," he says. "I am trying very hard. I am trying to work only 40 or 50 hours per week.

"The passion is the challenge of it," Henikoff says. "Because I require a certain amount of challenge in my life, I get it either from my business or I start seeking challenge elsewhere." Henikoff likes the thrill of the start-up.

"When you are creating something out of nothing, you are doing it quickly," he says. "Many times it involves bubblegum and duct tape. [As the business matures] you don't want duct tape and bubblegum, you want red tape, process and procedure.

"It was tough to hand over the reins because SurePayroll was my baby," he says. "I had programmers who programmed it. Every single aspect of it, I was actively involved in. It is hard to give up control.

"It is not about the money," he says. "I do it for the challenge and because I love it. I have this addiction.

"It's all about challenge. I rise to the challenge," he says. "In my experience, if you look at people who are entrepreneurs, you will find that in their personal life, a high percentage of them are doing things that are challenging.

"I love to create something out of nothing," he says. "You're like an alchemist."

A T *r u e* T *a l e*

DEAN RUTTER
How Financial Disaster Makes Baby Laugh

In 1995, Dean Rutter signed a term sheet for VC funding for Apartments.com. In 1996, he received venture funding, before just about anyone else in Chicago had. In 1997, he sold his business for $7.5 million to Classified Ventures. By then the venture investment had diluted his ownership, but still he had a chunk of change that he needed to invest. He tried a professional money manager. That didn't work out, so he invested the cash in CDs that earned a good rate at an Internet bank, Next Bank.com. The FDIC took receivership of the bank on February 7, 2002. Rutter lost a lot of cash.

Rutter took two weeks to think about what to do.

"I think I had a positive response to a significant financial loss," Rutter says. "I started a new business." His new start-up is called Make Baby Laugh.

Make Baby Laugh is inspired by Rutter's son, who was born in the year 2000. Rutter says, "The products include videos that entertain, build stronger family bonds using laughter, and help parents develop their kids' sense of humor."

Rutter is charging into the fatherhood business in a big way.

"He is obviously the light of my life," Rutter says. "And among all the things in my life that are wonderful, his laughter is something that I cherish. And it helps that I consider myself fairly creative about making my son laugh."

Rutter says he thought about getting a job but he prefers to work for himself because the success or failure of the venture rests squarely on his shoulders. "I have no fear of failure or of making a mistake. I have a fear of failing because folks I am beholden to don't grasp that success requires making 'smart mistakes.'

"The bottom line is that I started working on this two weeks after I lost the money. I spent a month trying to talk myself out of it. I could not find anything out there like this."

Rutter was highly encouraged when he mentioned his idea to a golfing buddy. His friend said that he had a similar idea.

"He said to me that there is no product out there that is about making your child laugh," Rutter says. "Sure, there are dozens of products that offer passive entertainment. But I was not able to find a single product whose goal is to help parents more effectively engage with their children and to make them laugh.

"I did my legwork on this and part of the reason I chose this youngest group is because of the relative lack of the niche's maturity," Rutter says. "I am a business guy first and foremost. I am a loving dad, and I have what I consider a very good idea. And I want to make money with this so I try to go where no one else has gone."

Rutter strongly believes that no business is unique. He went about learning everything he could about the market, including investigating Baby Einstein, which in about six years sold three million products.

Rutter says that the clincher came when Make Baby Laugh passed his "viability test," a list of roughly 50 questions he asks himself whenever he evaluates a new business opportunity. "If it works I will have created six to eight titles.

"Make Baby Laugh is an idea that has a relatively rapid liquidity horizon (five years) and the capital investment is modest. I have a whole rationale," Rutter says. "In the end if it goes south, I can say, 'OK, based on the information I had at the time, here's why I did this.' That's really what it is all about—making good decisions with limited information.

"To be cut from the entrepreneurial cloth means you have to be able to live and be comfortable with risk. It doesn't mean you have to be a risk junkie. But you have to feel OK that you are doing everything you can, that you are being as smart as you can, and that you are making the right decisions with the information you have.

"One of my big lessons in life is if you are going to fail, fail at something you don't mind failing at. In the end, what am I doing? I am creating a product that is intended to help parents bring joy and laughter to kids," he says.

"And you know what, this is a great way to spend my time."

You will never know if you have what it takes to be a "happily successful" entrepreneur. This way of making a living fits well into my life after traveling the road for the past 15 years. Does it work for you? You will not know until you take the journey and make it your own way.

You can ask yourself if you can be happy doing something else besides starting and growing your own business. If you can, go enjoy doing it. Can you handle traveling the roller coaster up and down with your family and friends? If no, then don't even get on the ride. Finally, no matter how hard you work, can you accept business outcomes even though they are well beyond your control? If you don't want to keep company with luck and fate, then don't start on this adventure.

If you have never done it before, don't expect honest answers from yourself. Without actually doing it, it is all really academic. But if you do take the leap, you will recognize the experience when it does come up and know the questions to ask.

If you think that starting and growing a business is hard, you are right.

If you think that it will take a long time, you are right.

If you think that you can fail, you are right.

If you think that you can fulfill your passion this way, you are right.

If you think that you can build something you can be proud of, you are right.

You are not alone on this journey. Although the market economy does not care about you, plenty of people will be there to help. Ask your family, friends, mentors, team, customers, and vendors to pitch in. You will be surprised at how they will come to your aid. Through perseverance, you will find your own way and achieve your own definition of success.

The businesspeople who are featured in this book are not meant to be a sampling of the greatest entrepreneurs of all time. While some of them may qualify for that status on many lists, each one is amazing in his or her own right. They are all real businesspeople. They have all been there and have struggled with business issues and the entrepreneurial lifestyle. I salute all these individuals who I consider to be our true captains of industry.

John Banta

As President and COO, John was out on an IPO road show for his company, Digitalworks, on April 14, 2000, when the stock market crashed. The firm was presenting to financial analysts right after Krispy Kreme Doughnuts. The doughnut company went public, Digitalworks did not.

As CEO/Managing Director of IllinoisVENTURES, John now provides leadership to a team that will develop and provide a broad array of mentoring and business development services for promising, high-potential new companies based on University of Illinois technologies.

Suzi Bonk

Suzi is a driving entrepreneurial force behind Winnipeg's business community. I met her a few years ago when I was asked to speak at Manitoba's premier economic conference.

Growing up in Africa, the United Kingdom, and North America, Suzi had a global upbringing that has allowed her to form international business partnerships, exchanges, and relationships. After a few successes and a number of failures, Suzi's private entrepreneurial interest currently is Sofa Logic Inc., a consultancy firm. Suzi founded TechMadness in 1999 to stimulate cooperation and camaraderie among Winnipeg's digital community. She has been nominated for the Women Entrepreneur of the Year Award three consecutive years.

Richard Cohen

Richard was married Memorial Day weekend 2003. He continues to strive to balance his entrepreneurial drive with his dedication to supporting his family. He is cofounder of Three Color Films, Inc. Richard has written and directed one short film, *Behind Your Eyes,* and has written a feature screenplay. He currently is developing three short films that are described on his Web site.

Stephanie Covall-Pinnix

I have been fortunate to know Stephanie during the past few years. She is an amazing businesswoman who always seeks to connect people to one another without regard to personal gain. I admire how she survived difficult family beginnings in Yakima to become truly part of the glue that holds the Chicago technology community together.

She is currently the Director of Business Development for SGS Net, an integrated marketing company. Stephanie is responsible for creating and driving the company's business development, sales, and marketing initiatives. Prior to SGS Net, she was the CEO of Triton-Tek, a Chicago-based company that specializes in scalable, custom-designed business solutions.

Alison Doree

Alison is driven to make the world a better place for people to meet and share their common experiences. Since March 2002, Alison has been developing the business plan, organizing a management team, and raising capital to launch Social League. In 1999, Alison founded UniteAmerica.net, Inc., a forum for online political discourse. Alison has been both an independent broker and company field sales representative in the consumer products industry.

Mike Duda

I met Mike while sharing office space with his company. He enjoyed a great international career at Arthur Andersen before starting Pennant, a hosting and maintenance business. Mike is driven every day to make his clients and team members productive and profitable. The only time he rested last year was to marry his bride in South America. He forgot his cell phone at home.

Vicki Esralew

Vicki, a nationally recognized parenting expert, speaks on the effects of today's often violent media on children. She advocates solutions to empower children and families through her company, Vickilew. I have watched Vicki for more than a year tirelessly advance her ideas through a journey of passion, laughter, tears, and perseverance. She has developed award-winning multimedia products from which to springboard this good for children mission.

Her Potty Training Product, "I Gotta Go," has been a leading seller at Wal-mart. I even can be heard occasionally singing the tunes from the CD.

Troy Henikoff

Long before I met Troy, I had heard about his successes as an entrepreneur. Back in Boston, in 1986, he started a small consulting firm with $1,000 and an answering machine. Years later, he sold the business to Medline, the largest privately held national manufacturer and distributor of health care supplies and services. He met Regis Philbin while he was at Jellyvision building the game version of "Who Wants to be a Millionaire" in only eight weeks.

Troy started SurePayroll with two other partners four weeks before he got married. In 2002, when the organization grew too big for him to operate, he replaced himself with a professional CEO. He now spends most of his time in the basement, dreaming up his next adventure.

Ari Kaplan

From baseball to software, Ari has shown he can do just about anything he wants. He is currently the cofounder and CEO of Expand
Beyond Corporation, a worldwide leader in mobile software for IT
management. Ari received his bachelor's degree in engineering from
the California Institute of Technology. In 1997, he was awarded the
school's prestigious Alumni of the Decade distinction.

In 2001, he was included in Crain Communications Inc.'s "40 under
40" profile of business leaders. Ari serves on the board of directors for
the International Oracle Users Group, the Chicago Software Association, and the *Talent Economy*, a national magazine for IT professionals.

Randy Komisar

Randy is one of my favorite authors. I have bought at least 50 copies
of his book *The Monk and the Riddle* to give to entrepreneurs who I meet
so they can understand what building a business is all about.

He works with emerging technology companies and social ventures, partnering with entrepreneurs to build strong businesses from
their vision. Randy is currently a Consulting Professor of Entrepreneurship at Stanford University.

Randy has helped guide companies such as WebTV, TiVo, Mondo-
Media, and Full Audio. He was President and CEO of LucasArts Entertainment Company, George Lucas' video game and edutainment
business. Randy was a founder of Claris Corporation, a developer and
publisher of productivity software. Later he served as CFO and VP Business Operations for GO Corporation, the pioneer in pen computing.

Kay Koplovitz

Kay is an amazing force behind Springboard Enterprises, a women's
venture-capital forum where more than 250 companies have raised
more than $1 billion.

Kay is the founder of USA Network, the Sci-Fi channel, and USA
Networks International, a company launched in 1977. She served as
Chairperson and CEO until the company was sold for $4.5 billion in
1988. She is currently a principal of Koplovitz & Co., LLC. She is the

author of *Bold Women, Big Ideas* (May 2002), which she wrote to inform and inspire women entrepreneurs to create wealth through equity.

Jack Kraft

Jack is one of Chicago's wisest business advisors. From guiding large corporations to start-up ventures, Jack has experienced it all. He honed his strategic and leadership skills at Leo Burnett, where he participated in the development, management, and significant growth of the legendary agency, whose operations encompass 50 offices in 43 countries and nearly 7,000 employees worldwide. At the time of his retirement from Burnett, Jack was COO and a member of the Executive Committee and Board of Directors.

Jack was founder and advisor of interactive marketing services providers Two-Way Communications and Modem Media. As prominent in philanthropic and civic circles as he is in business, he serves on the board of advisors of the College of Liberal Arts and Sciences of DePaul University and is a member of the Finance Committee of Lawson House YMCA.

Jim Lichtenstein

I met Jim during the Internet heydays when he had built an incredible site for newsrooms with $100 worth of software on his home computer. Jim began his career in the newsroom of ABC/WLS-TV in Chicago. For most of his 18 years at ABC, he was the Assignment Editor, winning a number of awards, including two Emmys.

In 1993 he left news to produce the *Bertice Berry* talk show for Twentieth Century Television. In 1996, Jim created and was Executive Producer of the ABC Sunday Night Movie *Talk to Me*. In 1997, he returned to news at CBS/WBBM-TV as Managing Editor. In October of 2000, Jim left CBS to become the full-time CEO of AssignmentEditor.com. The site was sold to MediaMap, Inc. in December of 2002.

Sean Lundgren

I have never personally met Sean although I feel like I know him. He found my hacker Web site on the Internet a year back and we started to share our business ideas over the phone and via e-mail. His experiences show that the truth of operating a small business is always scarier than we can ever make up. I admire his perseverance, bravery, and hope.

He recently closed Smeetch.com, which he had built from a $50-per-month Yahoo! store to $4 million in sales of DVDs, VHS, video games, music, and books. He was briefly able to regain profitability but another technology problem killed his company in May 2003. His house is up for sale and all his family's savings and investments are gone. He is currently looking for a job. Sean sincerely hopes that others can learn from his odyssey.

Rick Mazursky

Over the past year, Rick has become one of my favorite mentors. I can always count on him as my "business ethics" meter to guide me to do the right thing even when I get off course. He has 35 years of experience in product design and development, marketing, and domestic and international distribution. Rick has held leadership positions in companies involved in the creation and distribution of products to consumers and has served as President of Vtech Industries.

Rick has served on the following boards of directors: Vtech Industries, Inc., The Toy Manufacturers of America, The Midwest Toy Association, the Board of Advisors of Leap Frog Enterprises. He has been inducted into the Entrepreneurship Hall of Fame and nominated for the Ernst & Young Entrepreneur of the Year Award. He has been awarded five U.S. patents.

Marsha McVicker

I have always admired Marsha's passion and undaunted dedication to her business endeavors. As Errand Solutions' founder and CEO, Marsha has a solid background in supply chain management, communications, strategy, and channel development.

Her experience includes work as a consultant to the transportation industry and more than six years as a communications director on Capitol Hill in Washington, D.C. While completing her Supply Chain Management and Entrepreneurship MBA from the University of Wisconsin–Madison, Marsha was able to develop the approach to her company.

Matt McCall

Whenever I am on a business panel discussion with Matt, I do not talk (which is hard for me), I just listen. I just write down what he says because he is always so insightful. He is a cofounder and Managing Director of Draper Fisher Jurvetson Portage Venture Partners and is a partner at Portage Venture Partners.

Matt has served on the advisory board to Mayor Daley's Council of Technology Advisors in Chicago as well as on numerous other regional high-technology advisory boards. He is also a founding board member of Atomworks, a regional nanotechnology consortium. He has been honored by *Crain's Chicago Business* on its annual "40 under 40" list of leading Chicagoans under age 40. He is a founder and trustee of the McCall Family Foundation, focused on improving early childhood development in Chicago's disadvantaged communities.

Bob Okabe

In my mind, Bob is almost always the smartest guy in the room. I depend on him constantly to explain technology and complicated financial models to me. He is a corporate executive whose clients have ranged from Fortune 500 companies to three-person start-ups. During the past 20 years he has worked in every aspect of financial and general management from cost accountant to chief financial officer.

Bob is currently a principal of Illinois Partners, a consulting firm specializing in strategic and financial advisory services for technology and growth companies. Among its clients are the Illinois Technology Enterprise Center at the Argonne National Laboratory. With me, Bob is also one of the founders of Prairie Angels Capital Partners, LLC, the manager of the first organized angel fund in the Chicago area.

David Ormesher

Dave is a pillar of the Chicago entrepreneurial community. He has built a business that is equally respected by his employees, customers, and vendors for the past 16 years.

As CEO of Closerlook, Dave provides strategic direction and leadership for company. He has taken Closerlook from a small, creative media boutique and grown it into a recognized leader in creating innovative communication solutions that help clients in the pharmaceutical and technology industries. Dave has more than 20 years' experience in marketing communications. He began his career in the television industry and served as journalist and producer for a syndicated, magazine-format series entitled *A Closer Look.*

Mohnish Pabrai

Mohnish is a visionary in both business and finance. He is admired for knowing when to start and when to quit. From 1990 to 1999, Mohnish was the founder and CEO of TransTech, a bootstrap start-up. The company grew to $20 million-plus in revenue with 160 people when it was sold in 2000. TransTech was recognized as an *Inc.* 500 company in 1996.

Mohnish is the Managing Partner of the Pabrai Investment Funds, a close replica of the original 1950s Warren Buffett Partnerships. He is the winner of the 1999 KPMG High Tech Entrepreneur award.

Manish Patel

Manish is a business warrior. He has had to withstand one of the toughest conflicts with a partner that I have witnessed. He has survived this long encounter and is now thriving by running the business on his own.

He is CEO of Where2GetIt, a premier provider of intelligent location-based marketing services geared toward channel development companies. Manish's client service and management philosophies have enabled the company to grow its customer base to more than 280 clients and 130 consumer brands that include Polaroid, La-Z-Boy, Mitsubishi, and Reebok.

Penny Pickett

I have never met Penny although I know and admire other members of her firm. She serves as the Business Director for the Telecommunications Development Fund (TDF). Prior to joining TDF, Penny served as senior advisor to the deputy administrator of the U.S. Small Business Administration (SBA). While at the SBA, she was instrumental in developing the Equity Matters Seminar Series as well as the SBA-Federal Reserve cooperative workshops on access to capital for women and minority-owned businesses.

As the founding partner and owner of a small business, Penny spent more than 12 years building a company that combined traditional graphics production and design with innovative technological tools.

Dean Rutter

Dean's energy and enthusiasm for business is evident within the first five minutes of meeting him. I am convinced that his passion never leaves him time to breathe. He is an experienced entrepreneur, business leader, and decision maker.

Dean recently launched his second start-up, Make Baby Laugh!, a children's products business. Previously he consulted start-up companies in the areas of strategy, fundraising, technology, business development, operations, and sales. Dean also founded and sold Apartments .com where he served variously as Chairman, President and Chief Operating Officer, and Chief Technology Officer.

Liz Ryan

Liz has done the impossible by building the largest connected discussion community for women, WorldWIT, with more than 25,000 subscribers in 20 countries.

Liz is a former Fortune 500 corporate executive, an entrepreneur, and author and speaker on at-work issues. Liz and WorldWIT have been profiled in *Time* magazine, *Fortune* magazine, *The New York Times*, and *The Wall Street Journal* and on CNN. Liz lives in Boulder, Colorado, with her husband and five kids, ages nine months to nine years.

Natalie Tessler

I was moderating a business panel that Natalie was participating in a few years ago. I soon became a regular client at her business, Spa Space. I have come to respect how she has grown her company over the past two years through an uncompromising dedication to client service.

Her day spa located in downtown Chicago offers a corrective, clinical approach to spa services in a luxurious, nurturing environment. Natalie's professional experience includes working as a tax associate at the New York firm of Battle Fowler, and as an estate and financial planning associate at the Chicago firm of Katten Muchin Zavis Rosenman. Natalie regularly speaks to students, entrepreneurs, and angel investors on the topics of capital raising, business plan development, and entrepreneurship.

Jodi Turek

From watching her parents run their bagel restaurant in Brooklyn, Jodi has become a driving spirit behind Womensforum.com and Teens forum.com.

A former television reporter and news/talk show producer, her ability to attract entrepreneurial yet "everyday" women who are making a difference forms the backbone of Womensforum.com's unique Partner Network. She has 17 years of broadcast, print, public relations, and new media experience and speaks regularly about leveraging the power of women online.

David Weinstein

I met David only after he had achieved a lot of success at the Chicago Mayor's Office and then failed when his company, BlueMeteor, went out of business. Now in his early 30s, he has survived the roller coaster and is thriving again.

David is the first president of the Chicagoland Entrepreneurial Center. He oversees all day-to-day operations of a large regional base of entrepreneurs. Previously, David was president and CEO of BlueMeteor, a technology firm he helped launch and grow to $5 million in revenue with 110 employees. At BlueMeteor, he led the firm in successfully raising $30 million of venture capital. Earlier, he pioneered the position as Chicago Mayor Richard M. Daley's senior technology advisor.

Alexander, Caroline. *The Endurance.* Alfred A. Knopf, 1999.

Hawken, Paul. *Growing a Business.* Fireside, 1988.

Komisar, Randy. *The Monk and the Riddle.* Harvard Business School Press, 2001.

Koplovitz, Kay. *Bold Women, Big Ideas.* Public Affairs, 2002.

Peppers, Don, and Martha Rogers. *The One to One Future: Building Relationships One Customer at a Time.* Currency/Doubleday, 1997.

Schultz, Howard, and Dori Jones Yang. *Pour Your Heart Into It.* Hyperion, 1999.

Sinetar, Marsha. *Do What You Love, the Money Will Follow.* DTP, 1989.

Whyte, William, Joseph Nocera, and Jenny Bell Whyte. *The Organization Man.* University of Pennsylvania Press, 2002.